Paul Sutcliffe

H IGH AND D RY

Limited Special Edition. No. 16 of 25 Paperbacks

Author on Sonic Boom in the BVI

Paul was a university lecturer when he decided to buy a sailboat and find a different way of living. During the voyage, he kept a blog that received over 55,000 hits and had two articles published in the magazine *Sailing Today*.

Paul Sutcliffe

HIGH AND DRY

AUSTIN MACAULEY PUBLISHERS™
LONDON · CAMBRIDGE · NEW YORK · SHARJAH

Copyright © Paul Sutcliffe (2019)

The right of Paul Sutcliffe to be identified as the author of this work has been asserted by him in accordance with section 77 and 78 of the Copyright, Designs and Patents Act 1988.

All rights reserved. No part of this publication may be reproduced, stored in a retrieval system, or transmitted in any form or by any means, electronic, mechanical, photocopying, recording, or otherwise, without the prior permission of the publishers.

Any person who commits any unauthorised act in relation to this publication may be liable to criminal prosecution and civil claims for damages.

A CIP catalogue record for this title is available from the British Library.

ISBN 9781528928625 (Paperback)
ISBN 9781528965569 (ePub e-book)

www.austinmacauley.com

First Published (2019)
Austin Macauley Publishers Ltd
25 Canada Square
Canary Wharf
London
E14 5LQ

Thank you to the following people who helped kickstart this project:

                        Steven Jungk
                        Susan Sutcliffe
                        Helen Sutcliffe
                        Sally Sutcliffe
                        Jane and Mick Bird
                        Erin Deighton
                        Elsa Ward
                        Andrew Hardy.

Back cover photo: Author with the Simon Morris sculpture 'Guardian of the Reef' in Grand Cayman.

Cover photo: Sonic Boom anchored in Oracabessa, Jamaica

Table of Contents

Introduction   **10**

Chapter 1   **12**
The British Virgin Islands

Chapter 2   **22**
St Martin

Chapter 3   **34**
The Lesser Antilles

Chapter 4   **41**
Trinidad

Chapter 5   **52**
The ABC Islands

Chapter 6   **69**
Jamaica

Chapter 7   **75**
The Cayman Islands

Chapter 8   **105**
Hispaniola

Chapter 9   **112**
   The Virgin Islands

Epilogue   **116**

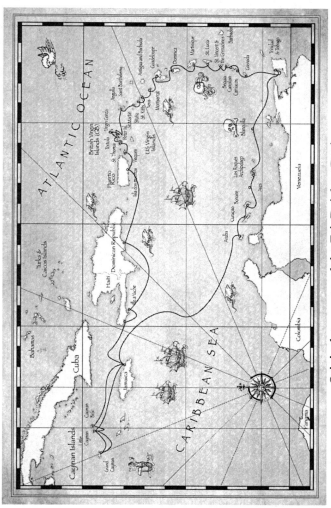

Original map artwork by ErinDeightonDesign

Introduction

Have you ever dreamed of mooring your own yacht in turquoise seas of white sandy beaches? Spending lazy days in the sun, drinking coconuts on the beach, or snorkelling over the coral reefs? I was a university professor in California when I decided to take a chance and go and try to live more simply in the Caribbean. It wasn't that I wanted to escape the endless chase of consumerism so much, rather I wanted to discover a wholly different way of life, one more in tune with nature. I sold everything I owned, cashed in my pension and booked a flight to the British Virgin Islands.

I had been to the Caribbean before; to Barbados, Tortola, St Maarten and Antigua, but I usually stayed in expensive resorts. I wanted a more sustainable way to travel around the islands. I decided to buy a boat and sail. I'd learnt to sail on big eighty-foot yachts around the UK when I was a small boy, but I wasn't an expert sailor. I did some more sailing in Monterey Bay and took offshore and blue water sailing exams to get up to date, and so I could qualify for cheaper boat insurance.

Using the wind as my main energy source, I planned to keep living expenses to a minimum. I had no mortgage or rent and my electricity was free. I had no monthly bills. All I needed was food and a little cooking gas. I would try to pick up work wherever possible. I could crew on other yachts, charter my own boat, work in boatyards, or maybe teach some English. I would try anything.

I wanted to cruise the islands for as long as I could, forever if possible and visit as many islands as I could. First, I would head to Trinidad, stopping at all the islands on the way. From there, I would head west along the Venezuelan coast to the ABC islands, then north to Jamaica; although, I would be flexible and change plans depending on the circumstances.

This is the story of the first four years of that adventure; a journey of over three thousand miles covering the whole Caribbean Sea, visiting more than forty islands. I encountered pirate attacks, tropical storms and hurricanes, ripped sales and engine failures. I also discovered a sailing community, making lifelong friendships along the way. I will start in Tortola, in the British Virgin Islands, since that is where I bought my boat.

Chapter 1
The British Virgin Islands

The first thing I needed to do was buy a boat, so I booked a trip to Tortola and made appointments with yacht brokers there. Until I had my own boat, I stayed in the cheapest hotels I could find, hitching rides around the island. I started looking at fairly new ex-charter boats, with BVI Yacht Brokers who were based in Nanny Cay, a small bay and marina.

The British Virgin Islands is one of the most popular sailing destinations in the world, and the many marinas and bays are full of thousands of boats. There are four main islands and over fifty smaller ones, all within a day's sail. The numerous islands allow the trade winds to pass but stop the waves, making ideal sailing conditions. A number of very large charter companies are based there and they periodically sell their boats off as they replace their fleet with new ones, meaning it is also a great place to get a cheap boat.

I liked hitching in the BVI, lots of people stop, and they were usually interesting. There weren't many buses, and taxis were really expensive. I started by just sticking my thumb out, but apparently there that's like sticking your middle finger out. What you should do is point to the road and the direction you want to go. Once in Tortola, an old man stopped for me, and when I thanked him, he said,

'Don't tank me, tank da lard, was 'is decision for me to stap.'

He was such a nice old guy and took me all the way to the airport. Another time, I got a cool dreadlock Rasta wearing shades and with his seat way back so that he was almost horizontal. He stopped, opened the door, didn't say anything, just nodded and played music full blasting from at least eight speakers, the heavy base making the whole car vibrate. After he dropped me off, I could still hear his music as he disappeared over a hill.

I spent a few days looking at boats. I wanted something under forty feet that would be easy to sail single-handed and cheap to maintain. I found a 2005 Beneteau 343 which I liked. It had a luxury white leather interior, two large cabins and a separate shower, and would be great for chartering. However, there was no way I could afford it, so I started looking at older boats and focused on the essentials: the hull, the engine and the rigging – these are the important parts.

Older boats, pre-1980, are generally much better made than modern boats. They are heavier, made with thicker fiberglass and often have full keels. I realised that it was possible to buy a better boat for much less money. However, not many yacht brokers list them since the lower prices meant less commission. The problem was how to find a good one that was for sale. I looked at the classifieds in the local newspaper, *The BVI Beacon*, but didn't find much, so I persisted with the brokers and went to see a 1980s Beneteau First, one of the few boats they had listed that was in my budget.

The boat was moored at Manuel Reef Marina. The photos had looked good, but when we got there, we found the boat was badly damaged. It had been smashed against the dock, the toe rail was hanging off and the fiberglass was cracked and ripped along the deck seam. Rainwater had leaked into the cabin. I wondered how much all that would cost to fix.

'Could be five thousand, could be fifteen,' said the broker, without much enthusiasm. Then his eyes lit up and he said,

'*That* is the boat you should get,' pointing to a slip further down, and a pale blue boat tied up to it. It wasn't one of their listings, but a boat that he had seen before. He'd tried to convince his girlfriend to buy it. It was still for sale and he had the owner's number.

I called and arranged to meet the owners and have a look around. It was a very rare 1969 Elizabethan 31 sloop, painted an unusual but beautiful Bahama blue. Built in England, originally marketed as a "gentleman's cruiser", it was thirty-one feet long, very heavy, with a full keel and designed to deal with the rough seas of the English channel. The thicker hull and the full keel meant it would handle heavy seas much better and I wouldn't be limited to the Caribbean; I could sail across the Atlantic if I wanted. Although slightly less manoeuvrable in small marinas, it was my plan to avoid marinas and their fees as much as possible anyway.

The Elizabethan had been surveyed less than two years ago, which would satisfy insurance companies and meant I didn't need to pay over a thousand dollars for another one. I took it for a sea trial with the owner and was happy. It had fairly new sails in good condition and all the rigging looked good. It had a 1998 Yanmar diesel engine, also in good condition, a Garmin chart plotter and a VHF radio. It came with an old beat-up dinghy and a tiny old Johnson outboard. So I fell in love with an Elizabethan 31, a boat very similar to the Contessa 32, which was my dreamboat. It was solid and uncomplicated which would hopefully mean it would be easier and cheaper to maintain. I had read many articles about what type of boat is best for single-handed budget cruising and was happy with what I'd got. I registered her as a small UK ship, renamed *Sonic Boom*.

Inside was not so good, and nothing like the newer luxury interiors I'd been looking at. There was a cabin in the bow which was pretty basic, a small rusty propane stove was on the point of being dangerous, the seating arrangement in the salon was uncomfortable and cramped and there was a huge fridge strapped down taking up all the room. I was worried that this was going to be where I would live but thought that with some work I could make it much better, and really I didn't have much choice.

At the beginning of November 2013, I moved aboard *Sonic Boom*. Everything I owned was with me in my sail bag. I was so excited, looking around the boat, checking everything out. The mooring at Manuel Reef Marina was paid for until the end of the month, so I spent my first week at the dock cleaning and checking systems and equipment. I painted my cabin and threw away lots of junk and old ropes I wouldn't need but *Sonic Boom* still seemed to be very small inside. Would I really be able to live in such a cramped space? I soon realised though that I had been looking at it like a house. Once I took it for a sail, everything made much more sense.

While I was docked at the marina, I made friends with my neighbours there. There was a guy with a dog living on his motor yacht on one side and a dentist from Alaska who part-owned his big Beneteau on the other. Every marina in the Caribbean seems to have an old pirate. At Manuel Reef it was Jim the manager.

He was an old sailor with a long, white beard and a big belly, a bit like Santa. I asked him if he'd ever made the crossing to St Martin.

'Ho, ho, ho a thousand times.'

'Is it difficult?' I asked.

'Ho, ho, ho, no, it's easy. Just sail over the horizon and then follow the lights to St Martin.'

My first passage was from Manuel Reef Marina, where the previous owners had the boat moored, round Tortola to Beef Island and Trellis Bay where I could anchor for free, and where there was a community of sailors living on their boats. I set off from the marina and tacked across the Sir Francis Drake Channel to Beef Island. As I approached the tip of Tortola, I noticed another boat about a mile behind me. I also noticed some very black clouds heading my way. I managed to tack and head towards Trellis Bay just before the squall hit. Behind me, the boat following disappeared in a massive rain shower. I laughed and shouted,

'I am awesome!' And then almost immediately got knocked down by another squall that I hadn't noticed because I was too busy looking behind. All of a sudden my mast was almost horizontal, the boom was in the water and I was struggling to stand up. Then, almost as quickly, *Sonic Boom* sliced through the water, righted herself, headed into the wind and came to a stop.

When I finally made it into Trellis Bay, I spent twenty minutes poking my boathook at various mooring balls until Trish, a lovely lady from Tasmania aboard a small motor cruiser, spotted me.

'Where'd you come from?' she shouted across the water. When I said England, she immediately jumped into her dinghy and came to help. I got tied up to a mooring ball, and she asked me how long it had taken. I checked the time and was very pleased, I proudly answered,

'Four hours.'

Trish, though, wasn't impressed. Horrified, she shouted,

'I thought you'd crossed from England.'

Trish soon left. I took a break, had a cup of tea and then moved off the buoy and dropped my anchor, feeling quite happy with a successful first passage.

At Trellis Bay, there were lots of people who lived aboard their boats, so it was a good place to meet people. The airport was only a short walk away and had clean toilets, power outlets and a café serving cheap local food. The best things, though, were swimming with turtles in the bay and the full moon parties, which featured the amazing fire sculptures of the local artist Aragorn, who had a studio there. One night, I was woken up by a concert on the beach. Ironically, they were singing: '*Don't wake me up, up, up,*' but it sounded great so I dinghied over and joined in the fun.

On the other hand, there weren't many facilities, like showers or a launderette. I soon learnt that it was easiest to motor over to Marina Cay, a tiny little island only a mile or two away, which had a fuel dock, showers, launderette, a great restaurant, free Wi-Fi and good snorkelling. The anchorage, however, was very deep and on one trip I just didn't have the strength to heave in my anchor and all the chain. I did have a windlass on board but it wasn't fitted so I had to manually heave in my anchor. Luckily, another cruiser spotted me and probably slightly concerned about his own boat, which was close by, came over and helped me get it up.

After a few weeks, I left Trellis Bay and sailed to Peter Island for a couple of nights. I anchored in Deadman's Bay, behind Dead Chest Island, where Blackbeard marooned some of his crew. It was also the inspiration for *Treasure Island*. I was feeling more like a pirate. As I sailed into the bay, I could see *Tara*, a beautiful Hylas 54 owned by Mark and Lisa, an awesome couple from Oklahoma I'd met in Trellis Bay. Ten times as big, and a hundred times more valuable, it made me feel tiny. Later though, a crewmember on a chartered catamaran dinghied over just to compliment me on my Elizabethan 31.

'You've got the best boat in the bay,' he said, which made me feel good, although Mark wasn't too impressed.

On Peter Island, there's a luxurious resort. The football player Rio Ferdinand once hired the whole place for his wedding party. I had breakfast there with Mark and Lisa. Afterwards, we walked to the top of the hill and had spectacular views of nearly all the Virgin Islands. We could even see St Croix in the far distance. In the evening, they invited me aboard *Tara* and we had dinner together. They were an amazing couple, two of the nicest people I've met. I would run into them again and again as we all headed south, island hopping down the chain.

Life in the Virgin Islands was lots of fun. Jost Van Dyke was my favourite island. I loved White Bay, and Ivan's campground, which was a great place with little wooden huts on the beach, and the Soggy Dollar Bar which was another good place to meet other sailors and drink painkillers – a rum cocktail made with orange and pineapple. I liked to hike over the hill from White Bay to Great Harbor, where there were some amazing views.

Hitching a lift from Great Harbour back over the hill to White Bay one day, I met a lovely girl called Arianna. It turned out her mum worked at Ivan's and agreed to give me a ride in her new truck. I chatted with Arianna, who told me she was five while we waited for her mum to collect some take-away fried chicken. Then just as we were setting off, Arianna was sick. Apparently, her dad had given her shrimp for breakfast, which she threw up into her hands trying to catch it all, but it went all over the front seat. I got out and helped her clean her hands and face with a bottle of water I had while her mum angrily cleaned up the car. So we became friends and I spent a few days hanging out with Arianna while she was off school poorly, building sandcastles and having fun.

Looking through a sailing magazine one afternoon, I recognised a picture of a huge motor yacht I had seen off Norman Island. At the time I thought it was ugly. It was an enormous catamaran that I thought looked like Tupperware. Then I noticed it was a Feadship, a very expensive Dutch make of super yacht, and thought it must have a famous owner. It turned out to be *Venus*, the boat Steve Jobs commissioned, and the designer Philip Stark tried to impound for unpaid fees.

Although I felt like I could have stayed there forever, BVI was quite an expensive place and the job opportunities were limited. Plus, I was also eager to set sail. I planned to sail to St Martin, so I first needed to get to Virgin Gorda, the best departure point for a sail across the dreaded Anegada Passage. I had an easy sail to Virgin Gorda, the wind had shifted to the south a little and I made it on one tack in just a few hours. When I got to Necker Island, home of Sir Richard Branson, I hove-to, dropped my sails and motored into North Sound, where I saw *Tara* again and went to say hello to Mark and Lisa.

I often heave-to on *Sonic Boom*. Heaving-to seems like it has become an old-fashioned sailing technique that isn't so popular anymore. For a single-handed sailor though, it's incredibly useful. Heaving-to is essentially a way of stopping the boat with the sails up, like parking in the middle of the ocean. When you tack, you turn the boat so the wind comes from the opposite side, and both sails swing over to the other side of the boat. When you heave-to, you stop the fore sail from swinging to the other side, so it turns itself inside out. Now it isn't giving any forward force anymore but still catches the wind and pushes the boat back and to starboard. On the other hand, the mainsail was allowed to swing over and gives a forward force, to port. The boat rocks forward then back as the two sails cancel each other out until it comes to a rest, balanced by opposite forces. Even in very strong winds, the boat doesn't move. Another strange thing is that when you're hove-to the sea off the stern quarter becomes calm, even in rough waves.

I stopped to fill up with water and anchored off Saba Rock, next to a beautiful white sandy beach. Behind it, there was a small lagoon with flamingos. Saba Rock is a tiny island, with a hotel, restaurant and a small white sand beach. Although it was quite expensive, like the rest of Virgin Gorda, it was lovely. There were old canons and huge anchors dotted around and the hotel shop sold recovered treasure from old wrecks. They also had a display of antique outboard engines. I thought mine wouldn't look too out of place.

Later, I met Mark and Lisa's German friends, Kerstin and Robert, on their amazing yacht *Trinity*, and two of their friends Nicole and Holger. They were real characters, Robert made me think of the Herman Hesse's *Steppenwolf*. They were on a round-the-world voyage of discovery. One night, we all had dinner together on Tara, which was fun. After a snorkel before dinner, Mark and I were on his swim platform and he handed me the shower. Hot water! It was the first hot shower I'd had in weeks. I didn't want to be rude and use too much of his precious water so after a couple of minutes I gave the shower back to him, but my hand didn't seem to want to let go. It was funny. Kerstin said it was like the scene in the film *Sleepers* where Woody Allen passes the orb around.

The main hotel on Virgin Gorda was The Bitter End Resort, a huge, very luxurious and expensive resort, which was actually more like a small village. In fact, it reminded me of The Village from the TV series *The Prisoner*. The staff rode around in little golf carts and waved at you as they passed. I half expected them to say "be seeing you". One day, I was sitting in one of the cafés surfing the Internet, checking the weather forecasts when I started having problems with my power cord. Another cruiser, a lovely lady called Sabrina who was on board *Honey Ryder,* came over and offered to help. She did help and we became friends. In fact, Sabrina and Tom would become two of my best friends and I would meet them many times over the next few years. Tom said that *Sonic Boom* reminded him of a 1960s British sports car. I hoped he was thinking more Jenson Interceptor and less MG Midget.

After a few nights anchored off Saba Rock, I moved across North Sound to anchor off Leverick Bay Resort for a while to check it out. It was much cheaper than Bitter End, not as luxurious but a lot friendlier. There were free showers, Wi-Fi, a launderette and a reasonable mini mart. There was also a nice swimming pool and a pretty little beach. While I was anchored just off their marina, a dinghy came up, the person on board introduced himself and offered to buy *Sonic Boom*. I told him it wasn't for sale and felt good about my boat.

One day, I walked from Leverick Bay up over the hill to Gun Greek. There was a cheap supermarket there, and I wanted to check where the immigration office was and see where I could anchor. Gun Creek has a fairly new immigration office – you could clear in and out, even though some of the tourist brochures said you couldn't. It was a long hike over a steep hill, but on the way back I managed to hitch lifts. Two rides that took me pretty much all the way. First, a local woman on her way to the post office took me half way. Then, an American guy took me, out of his way, right to Leverick Bay marina.

During my last few days in Virgin Gorda, it was so fun hanging out with Kerstin and Robert, laughing and chatting, swapping music and stories. Happy hour at Saba Rock, pizza at the Bitter End, afternoon tea on *Sonic Boom*, dinner on *Trinity*. What an amazing yacht that was. It was huge, made of aluminium and very high tech and couldn't be more different to

Sonic Boom. They helped me so much and they taught me so much, sharing all the things they'd learnt on their boat. A couple of times, they came on board *Sonic Boom*, looked around, and told me I needed to do this and this and fix that and that. Each time the next morning, I would do all the things they'd said needed doing. Eventually, they set sail for St Croix and I was so sad to say goodbye. It wouldn't be long though before I bumped into them again.

One day, dinghying back to my boat, I looked down and instead of dinghy's floor, I could see fish. It was a bad sign. In fact, the dinghy was beyond repair so I dumped it in a skip. Luckily, I managed to find a new one, with the help of Cyril (a taxi driver) I had met a few days earlier, for only a hundred and fifty dollars. Not really new, in fact, it was deflated on a beach and covered in dirt and full of ants. I spent a day cleaning it up, and patching the leaks, and transformed it into a nice Zodiac, which was much better than my old one.

After I had cleaned and repaired my new dinghy, I needed to borrow a foot pump, so I asked around but couldn't find anything. The only boat with people aboard that I hadn't asked was *Necker Belle*, Richard Branson's huge catamaran, that was taking on fuel and water at the dock. So I went over and asked them if I could borrow a foot pump. I managed to borrow Richard Branson's foot pump to blow up my dinghy which I thought was very cool and thought about not giving it back to him. I heard he was developing Mosquito Island into an eco-resort.

Although I had planned to leave on Christmas Eve, the weather forced me to wait. That meant I got to spend Christmas Day with my friends Mark and Lisa from *Tara*, who arrived at Leverick Bay on Christmas Eve. We had fun on the beach and then an amazing dinner at the restaurant. Sitting at the bar, I noticed Sir Richard Branson dinghy up and make his way to the restaurant. I said hello and we fist bumped. I was glad that I had given him his foot pump back after all.

Another day, I had been sitting in my boat when I heard someone shout,

'That's my old boat!'

The old owner, previous to the one I bought it off, was sailing into Leverick Bay marina on a catamaran. So I met him at the bar and chatted about the boat. He'd lived on it for a while, spent lots of money fixing it up and had been very sad to let it go.

I started to prepare for my next passage. St Martin was about eighty miles away, which meant sailing through the night across the Anegada passage. The Christmas winds were blowing hard and it was going to be rough. The wind would be almost dead against me, so too were the waves. This was going to be my first single-handed overnight crossing and I was excited, but also a little anxious. It was going to be unpleasant, scary even, but I knew the boat could take it. It should take about sixteen hours but would probably take me much longer. I planned to set off late morning with a reefed in main and jib. Hopefully, I could at least get near the coast of St Martin the next day, and then if I had to, I could motor sail the last few miles. Little did I know how wrong I would be.

Chapter 2
St Martin

Crossing the Anegada passage overnight, my biggest fear was being hit by a cruise ship, but I had lots of other mediums and small fears. I set off early in the morning and found it was painfully slow sailing all day. The wind was fairly light, but the waves and current against me were strong, so even though my sails seemed quite full, and the boat was smashing up and down, when I looked at the water, I was moving forwards but only very slowly. Two, maybe three knots at most. A dolphin came along and cheered me up, but I think it got bored with how slow I was going and left.

I sailed through the first night without sleep, and then all through the next day. I was tacking southeast and then northeast, trying to get east – but I just wasn't making much progress. On the second night, I finally arrived off the coast of St Martin in pitch darkness. There was a lot of boat traffic, so I decided to heave-to overnight, get a couple of hours' sleep and then try again in the morning. I bobbed around until dawn, with my lights on, trying to sleep but anxious of cruise ships, tankers and other boats.

The next day it was another hard slog. Eventually, I tried motoring, but there was something wrong with my engine. It kept accelerating uncontrollably, so I turned it off and started to make a plan to moor and anchor without it. I aimed for Long Beach, which looked easiest to get to and west facing which would make anchoring under sail easier. I tacked into the bay and when I got as close to the beach as I dared, I turned into the wind. As the boat slowed down and came to a stop, I quickly dropped my anchor, lowered my mainsail and furled in my foresail. As the wind pushed *Sonic Boom* away from shore, the anchor dug in. Perfect. After two days and nights of sailing, I'd made it. I wasn't exactly where I wanted to be but at least I was on St Martin.

Even though I was completely exhausted, I managed to get my dinghy in the water and attach the engine. I went to shore and headed to a beach bar. I saw there was a path leading to a very luxurious hotel high up on the cliff overlooking the beach. As I wandered up the path, I saw a hotel towel and grabbed it. As I came to the top of the path, I saw a beautiful infinity pool with views of the beach and the ocean. Everything was white marble and polished chrome. I had a shower and a dip in the pool and started feeling much better and a lot less salty. I finally made it to the bar and ordered the best beer and pizza I've ever had. I went back to the boat and slept for twelve hours straight.

The following morning I had to get my anchor up, without my engine and sail out of the bay. I headed for Marigot Bay, which was just a few miles along the coast, but it was incredibly hard. It felt like St Martin was blowing me away from every angle. The strong current and waves through the Anguilla passage meant it took me another five hours. I would later meet a couple who'd had similar problems to me. It had taken them five days, and even then they'd asked a fishing boat for a tow.

I arrived in St Martin with only five hundred dollars left. I desperately needed to find work, and quickly, otherwise this adventure would be finished before I'd even really got started. First I needed to check in with customs and immigration. Officially arriving boats should display a yellow quarantine flag once they enter that country's waters. Then only the captain is allowed ashore and must go straight to the customs office with the boat's registration papers and a copy of the clearance papers issued by the last port of call. Usually, you must pay a fee. Once the arrival papers have been stamped, you then go to immigration with your passport and those of anyone else on board. You then must pay another fee. Often there is also a port authority that also needs paperwork signing and a fee paying. When all that has been completed, the captain must go back to the boat, bring down the yellow flag and replace it with the national flag of the host country. Only then can everyone go ashore and grab a beer. I'd actually already done that, but I didn't mention that to the officials. The French were much more relaxed about clearing in and out, most of it was done on a computer, so I got away with it.

While I was in Marigot Bay, I arranged for a diesel mechanic to look at my engine, but they couldn't figure out the problem. I changed to oil and all the filters and the engine worked, so I motored through the bridge into Simpson Lagoon. To keep costs down, I used Sandy Ground Bridge which opens twice a day and is free, unlike the other bridge on the Dutch side. Mooring on the French side of Simpson's Lagoon was also free. The bridge opens only a couple of times a day. I went through the nine o'clock opening. It was fun in Marigot Bay with five or six other yachts all wanting to go in. We did a little dance, circling around, ready for the bridge to open, then waiting for the boats to come out, all lining up and motoring into the lagoon in a single file.

A blue crane lifted up a section of the road so the yachts could pass into and out of the French side of Simpson Lagoon. It was quite narrow, but the dredged channel you needed to follow all the way in was even narrower. Out of the channel, the lagoon is shallow, and I saw a couple of boats go aground and struggle to get off the bottom. As I approached Marina Port Le Royale and the quite small and crowded anchorage, I spotted a place I could go. Just as I dropped my anchor, another boat shouted at me,

'Stop! There's shallow, you're going to run aground,' but I already was stopping. Once I settled on the anchor, I was quite close to a few other boats but I didn't think it was a problem. It took me longer than expected to get there, but it was exactly where I'd planned to be.

Soon I had a visit from one of my neighbours. Francois, a huge old French pirate, with a grey beard and brown teeth came to see me in his underpants. Tight grey ones pulled up around his big belly. Actually, he looked more like a pro wrestler than a pirate.

'I think it is so nice you anchored so close to me,' he said with a smile.

After Francois, Eric, a weird-looking, stinky Dutch man, with even worse underpants, more like bikini bottoms shouted at me,

'You can't anchor there, you'll drag and crash into me.'

He was very grumpy.

Then another sailor came over on his dinghy. He asked me,

'Is this an Elizabethan 31?'

'Yes, but how did you know?'

He turned out to be a really nice guy, ex-merchant navy, who'd wanted to buy one in the 1970s but hadn't been able to afford.

That night was New Year's Eve and I had a great view of all the fireworks. I imagined they were for me celebrating my arrival.

I was next to a lovely English couple in a beautiful Gulf Star 54. Dane, who was from Barnsley, was a canvas expert and ended up fixing my dodger, the canvas cover over my cockpit. Amanda, his wife, was lovely, and they gave me lots of good advice. They told me how to avoid getting my dinghy stolen. Although even Dane questioned whether anyone would, reasoning that when you steal a dinghy, you need to make a quick getaway, which really wouldn't be possible with my tiny outboard. I could probably swim after anyone who tried.

Simpson Bay Lagoon was a strange place. I liked it because I was out of the waves, and it was an easy dinghy ride to pretty much everywhere. I liked being near Marigot and Port Le Royal, but the Dutch side was good too, and cheaper. Everywhere there was a mix of mega yacht marinas, expensive restaurants and five-star hotels, and rundown, old workshops and boatyards, half-sunken yachts and rusting old boats. Shipwrecks from a hurricane or just abandoned by the owner.

In the lagoon there were lots of very rich families and couples on two-week holidays, chartering luxury yachts like so many in the BVI, but it was also home for a large community of cruisers. There were sailors stopping off in the Caribbean on a circumnavigation, others who spent their time in the Caribbean sailing up and down the island chain. They were in St Martin for the cheap boat parts and services. A good place to meet them all was a bar called *Lagoonies,* which was next to the big chandleries Budget Marine and Island Water World on the Dutch side. On the French side there was *Spinnaker's*, another famous bar and very popular with sailors arriving from a trans-Atlantic crossing. The real pirates, though, all went to a place called *Cadisco's,* which was right across from where I was anchored.

Cadisco's was really a petrol station for cars, but it also had a dock for fuelling boats. Most importantly there was a mini mart that sold the cheapest beer on the island – one dollar (or one

Euro) for a bottle of *Carib*. This attracted a lot of old sailors from some very rusty, old boats dotted around the lagoon. There were a few picnic tables and benches outside that would fill up as the sun went down. I would go with Dane, say hello to Francois and listen to all their stories.

On the French side of the lagoon, there were lots of permanent live-aboards: old sailors, living on their own, camping in their boats. They didn't have much money either, but stayed afloat by fixing each other's boats and swapping parts. Lagoon monsters? Mostly they were lovely, kind and often offered to help or recommended someone who could. Lots of retired couples sailing long term on a budget. There was a cruisers' net on VHF every morning. There was also a flea market at Time Out Boat Yard every month, which was a great place to source cheap boat parts or maybe sell them to get some cash.

I call them pirates, but I don't mean that they are the same as the criminals attacking and robbing sailors off the coasts of Somalia or Venezuela or the real thieves in St Martin who'd steal your dinghy or come on to your boat at night. These old sailors were ex-merchant navy, or hippies who dropped out in the 1970s. Now they are old men with big bellies, beards, bad teeth, sometimes even one eye, who live on their boats and drink a lot of rum. They like to tell sea stories, get drunk and sing songs. Most of them are permanently anchored in St Martin, unable to fix their boats so they can move, but able to survive on an EU pension. They are usually grumpy but not dangerous and always interesting to talk to.

To help all the cruisers there was *Cruiser's Net* – a half-hour radio programme broadcast on VHF radio every morning. There are nets all over the Caribbean often run by other cruisers. In St Martin the net controller was Mike, an old Dutch guy that runs Shrimpy's. Shrimpy's, named after his dog, was a laundry and second-hand chandlery with its own dock on the side of the entrance channel to the lagoon. The net would start by inviting any newly arrived boats to say hello. That was followed by a weather report that was always very useful especially during hurricane season, which runs from June to November. There were also sections where cruisers could call in and ask for help or advice and a "treasures of the bilge" section where you could buy or sell old parts. I tuned in every morning, as did most other cruisers, and sometimes, it was very funny.

St Martin is one island split in two, half Dutch and half French. I first thought that the Dutch side would be most fun, but actually I ended up preferring the French side. The Dutch side had casinos and cruise ships. The French side had cheap breakfasts of croissants, coffee and orange juice and cheap baguette sandwiches for lunch. Marina Port Le Royale was a beautiful place to moor my dinghy and go shopping for provisions. There were lots of chic restaurants and bars around the marina, which was right in the middle of Marigot, the capital of the French side. I also found a nice beach and another nice hotel with showers and a pool.

I shopped at the cheap supermarkets and very rarely ate out at a restaurant. Supermarkets and bakeries had lots of good French food, bread, cheese and wine. There was also great Dutch food, chocolate, coffee and my favourite – stroopwaffels. Stroopwaffels are big round biscuits with a filling of caramel. They're big enough to rest on top of a cup of tea or coffee; you put the stroopwaffel on your cup of coffee like a lid to keep the coffee warm and melt the caramel inside.

St Martin was certainly much cheaper than the BVI. I would have *pain au chocolate* for breakfast with a coffee, orange juice and a banana. Lunch was usually a baguette sandwich and for dinner I made some pasta or a stir-fry with rice or noodles. I also followed *A Girl Called Jack's* blog for budget recipe tips. People often asked me what I ate, but really it was the same as normal. I had a functional galley with a sink and a stove. I did eat a lot of fruit, because it was easy and cheap to get in the Caribbean.

My engine still wasn't properly fixed. White smoke came out of my engine when I started it. I figured out that there was diesel getting into the oil but had no idea how. When I pulled out the dipstick, oil squirted out. Everyone I asked seemed to have a different idea. I took off my fuel injectors and had them checked by Global Marine Engine Servicing, who were awesome, but told me they were fine. They suggested the problem was my fuel pump. I took it off; the gasket had worn away, so I made a new one. However, I came to realise that replacing the fuel pump gasket would have had no effect at all. The problem would have to be the diaphragm, so I bought a whole new pump and replaced the old one. Budget Marine had one in stock for ninety dollars. Then I changed the oil and oil filter again for the third time in as many weeks. At least now the problem was properly fixed.

I managed to find work with Five Star Yachting Consultancy, and after my first week, I got paid. What a relief! My first job was helping the boss, Andy, restore two window frames for a motor yacht on the other side of the lagoon in Porto Copco. When they were done, we went to install them. It was fun to speed across the lagoon in his big powerful dinghy, which even had a steering wheel. It was very different to my dinghy.

Andy had his own dock outside the workshop and for a while I was allowed to tie up *Sonic Boom* there. It was actually very nice to be at a dock again for a few days, with shore power and water. I took advantage by scrubbing my decks and polishing the hull. I did as much as I could while I was there, lots of sanding, varnishing and painting. I was alongside Jock, an old pirate from Scotland, with a grey beard and a few brown teeth left. He twitched, had a big eye, and said "arr" and "matey" a lot, just like Captain Barbosa in *Pirates of the Caribbean*.

Jock was renovating an old shrimp boat, turning it into his new home. We became friends when I told him *Sonic Boom*'s homeport was Troon. He really started to warm to me though when I made him tea and gave him chocolate biscuits while we were both working on our boats. He told me with a tear in his eye how he'd lied about his age so he could join the merchant navy when he was fifteen and stories about smuggling rum in false fuel tanks around Jamaica and the Dominican Republic. In St Martin he worked as captain on a huge bright orange tug. Meeting him was one of the best parts of my stay in St Martin.

One day, we bumped into each other in the middle of the lagoon and drank a case of cold bears floating around in our dinghies, chatting and watching the sunset. We didn't have a bottle opener so Jock opened his first beer with his teeth, then handed me an unopened bottle with a smile to see how I'd open mine. I pretended to know a magic trick and opened it with my flip-flop and smiled back. Actually, I had a pair of Reef flip-flops that had a bottle opener on the sole, although I didn't tell Jock.

Jock's dinghy was a solid fiberglass skiff, rather than a "deflatable" like mine. Once we went to Barnacles, a cheap lagoon restaurant, and he tied up far away from the dinghy dock. I asked why he didn't tie up near the others.

'Tis a wee bit jagged,' he explained.

It was fairly beat up, the rope rub rail had mainly gone, leaving lots of bare fiberglass edge. It was very "pirate" and typical Jock. The water can get fairly choppy in the lagoon, and dinghies bump and bounce off each other while they're moored up. Once, he had tied it up like everyone else and came back to see all their dinghies shredded, bits of their rubber hanging off his. It caused a fair amount of trouble. I said it fit him perfectly.

I got some more days' work with Andy. He was busy and needed the help. I was sanding and varnishing a classic old sailboat, and then doing the same on *Sonic Boom* after work. I could use the yard's tools and some varnish I had on board. My teak was sanded, filled, sealed, bleached and varnished. I found there wasn't much teak left, it was nearly fifty years old and wearing thin. *Sonic Boom*'s hull was also clean and polished, although I'd discovered there wasn't really much paint left either. Inside I fitted new cushions and lights, and it was a much comfier place for lounging in the evening. I put in a new stereo and speakers and it sounded good. My soundtrack had been a small collection of CDs; The Skatalites' *Treasure Isle Time*, Little Roy's *Battle for Seattle* and Rihanna's *Unapologetic*, but I fixed my FM aerial, so I could also listen to the local radio stations. Reggae versions of *Hotel California* and steel drum band covers of Lionel Richie songs on Tradewinds FM. Helping to fix boats, I was learning how to fix mine. I was using my wages to pay for boat parts and food while trying to save some and not use my credit card.

I took my dinghy outboard out of the water and cleaned the carburettor. I also cleaned the fuel tank, and the engine, put it back together, oiled some bits and it was working much better. It was still only two horse power, but with it serviced, plus the new(er) dinghy, meant at least I'd got a much better set up than when I bought the boat. I still went slowly but I was much less worried about getting where I wanted to go. I went to the beach at Simpson Bay every day for swims in the morning and after work. I saw Steve Job's boat again, moored in Simpson Bay marina. Jock, the pirate, took me to a cheap local bar run by Chinese that did good egg and chips and had FA Cup football on the TV. It wasn't very Chinese, or Caribbean, but only five bucks with a beer.

My friends Sabrina and Tom arrived from the BVI on their yacht *Honey Ryder*. I met them and went to watch the fireworks for the opening of the new causeway that went right across the lagoon, French on one side, Dutch on the other. The French and the Dutch didn't seem to get along even though they were sharing a tiny island. Apparently, the French had refused to help finance the causeway bridge. On the VHF on the days leading up to the causeway opening, the Dutch port authority had been warning boats of the danger of the fireworks and announced an exclusion zone on the Dutch side. When a sailor asked about the French side, they said,

'We don't care, they can go as near as they like.'

It was a fun night.

Jock introduced me to a German guy who lived in St Martin who was looking to buy and live aboard an old sailboat. He'd only sailed Lasers, so wanted to get a feel for a boat my size. Jock had suggested going for a sail with me to see how he'd like it, so I had my first charter. I took Chris and Jock out in *Sonic Boom* for the day. We sailed all the way around St Martin in about seven hours. It was a great day's sailing with nice wind and a fairly calm sea, and I got a hundred and fifty dollars. I also got a compliment from Jock on my sailing that meant just as much. Although, I'd been serving him coffee laced with rum all day, so that might have had an effect.

On the way back I noticed a shroud had come free from the spreader, so we sailed the last part jib only and came back into the lagoon through the Dutch Bridge and then through the Causeway Bridge. A few days earlier, Amanda had been up the mast in the boson's chair to free a tangled line and had maybe dislodged or loosened a shroud fastening. I wasn't bothered, it was an easy fix. I just needed to tighten the standing rigging and fix stoppers over the spreaders.

We motored into and out of the lagoon and my engine was fine, having pumped out the oil with a hand pump, filled up with new oil and changed the oil filter, for the second time. I noticed though we were going slower than we should have been. The next day, I checked my propeller and it was covered in barnacles so I dove down and cleaned it. After, I stopped at Dane's on my way to have a hot shower and cleaned his too. He offered me money but I asked him to put it towards the cushion covers he had made me.

I insulated my fridge with Styrofoam and turned it down, so it was using less power. I was trying to get the fridge running on power just from my wind generator so I didn't have to keep running the engine to charge up my batteries. Really, I wanted a solar panel as well. The fridge was my main power consumer. Without it, the wind generator would make enough for everything – lights, GPS and depth gauge, fans and pumps. In the end I decided to give up and I put my fridge up for sale on the cruisers' net, run by Shrimpy's every morning on the radio. I got one call, but then sold it to Jock for a hundred dollars. I was glad to be rid of it. It was way too big for my boat. I wanted to get something smaller that my wind generator could power. I used the money to fix my wind generator, which was making so much noise, it sounded like a Spitfire was coming in to land on my deck. Something was definitely wrong with it.

Tom from *Honey Ryder* helped me take my wind generator down and dinghy it over to Mason, the wind expert in the lagoon, on his boat *Out of Africa*. Ironically, it was the only sailboat in the lagoon without a mast, but it made him easy to find. His boat was covered in machines and tools and looked like something from *Mad Max*. When we got there, Mason popped up from a hatch wearing round shades and welcomed us aboard. I gave him my generator and a week or so later he came over and helped me reinstall it. He'd completely rebuilt it; he changed all the bearings, cleaned it up and changed the blades. It was much quieter, although it was still a fairly noisy one, with low output. It was all I had though and at least should last a while longer.

I made friends with Baxter and Molly, an American couple, and went aboard their boat *Terrapin*, a Valiant 48. They were really fun, and their boat was one of the nicest I'd seen. Inside was absolutely beautiful. They had double beds, showers and beautifully varnished woodwork everywhere, even the engine was shiny. Outside was also immaculate. Later, they came aboard *Sonic Boom*. I don't think they were quite as impressed. Or else they were impressed by how I could live on such a boat. They came round again later and gave me a seat for my cockpit.

I got another charter. This time two English guys, Gavin and Andrew wanted to sail to Anguilla. We left on Tuesday and got back the following Thursday. We had a smooth sail to Anguilla, passing Sandy Island, which was a beautiful, tiny, sandy island. There was a small bar and good snorkelling. Afterwards, we continued to Road Bay, which was the place to anchor and clear in immigration. That charter meant another couple of hundred bucks and made it a thousand dollars I'd made in St Martin. I was just about managing to earn as much as I was spending. Most was going on food, the rest on laundry, showers, dinghy fuel and boat parts.

Approaching Road Bay I saw my friends Steven and Shawn on *Amaris* and anchored next to them. We had some wine on their boat and went for a hike. *Amaris* was a big Outremer catamaran that I'd first met in the lagoon in St Martin. It was gorgeous inside, very light and very fast. They'd bought it in France, sailed it across the Atlantic and were headed to Australia. I met them on the cruisers net – they'd radioed in an offer to help anyone that needed it with their US tax return forms. I did need help so I answered and we'd arranged to meet.

'I would like help with my tax return, last time I used H&R Block.'

'No problem, we own H&R Block, come over, we'll take a look.'

'I'm in the lagoon, near the Witch's Tit,' I said.

'So are we,' they radioed back.

'I'm anchored next to a huge great catamaran,' I said.

'Are you a little blue boat,' they asked, and when I said yes they said,

'We are that catamaran!'

So we both stuck our heads up out of our hatches and waved to each other.

One of my favourite things in St Martin was the flea market at Time Out Boat Yard. The first time I went, I bought a new foot pump and toilet seat. I had a Lavac toilet on *Sonic Boom*, which are very good. They're like an airplane toilet. The seat I bought was like new and still had a ninety-six-dollar price tag on it. I got it for two bucks. The pump was five. There was lots of junk, but lots of good stuff as well. Lots of cruisers and a few pirates hunting for bargains. My old neighbour Francois was there.

In Marigot I got to go to my first Caribbean carnival. There were dozens of floats making their way slowly through the town. Each float had its own sound system and DJs; thumping base, rocking tunes. The day after the carnival, my batteries were flat. I used all my battery water, bought some more and topped up my batteries. I had four fairly new house batteries on board that need topping up occasionally. I'd let the levels get way too low, but they seemed to be OK.

My friends Lisa and Mark were due to arrive on *Tara* at the end of the month, so I waited so I could see them, although I'd wanted to keep up with *Honey Ryder* who were leaving and were headed all the way to Trinidad, the same as me. However, I had another fun time with Mark and Lisa. We went to the Heineken Regatta party in Philipsburg. Then they left, headed to St Bart's and then Guadeloupe. The next day I watched the start of the races in Marigot Bay with a good view from Dane and Amanda's yacht, *Fairwinds of Teign*. After the races, I went from boat party to boat party and drank a lot of rum.

I got some more work cleaning propellers and scraping boat bottoms. I was also working with Amanda on their deck – priming and painting. We'd become good friends and I'd be very sad to say goodbye to Dane and Amanda. I'd already said goodbye to *Honey Ryder*. They'd gone to Antigua and were planning to be in St Lucia for the jazz festival in May. *Amaris* left too, it was also headed to St Lucia in May. It was sad waving goodbye to them too. I decided I should leave soon and catch up with everyone. So I slowly started getting ready to leave St Martin. I filled my propane tank for twelve dollars, the same as last time, three months ago. I also filled up with diesel, which was also fairly cheap, and forty gallons of water, which cost around fifteen cents a gallon. I went to the supermarket and stocked up on coffee and chocolate. My favourite supermarket was Simply – the Auchan supermarket on the French side.

Chapter 3
The Lesser Antilles

I finally left St Martin and had a good crossing to Statia. The thirty-five miles took about seven hours. I got to Oranje Bay, and there were lots of huge oil tankers anchored off shore. Two tankers anchored next to each other, bow to stern, is a huge obstacle to sail around and added an hour to my journey. Eventually, I picked up a buoy, had some food and went to bed. I didn't go ashore, so didn't check in or out of immigration. It wasn't that great, a very rolly bay, so I left early next morning before they opened and saved some money on fees.

The next day I had another good sail to St Kitts and Nevis. I got the sails just right and *Sonic Boom* pretty much went in a straight line. I was up to seven knots at times, but the wind was a little bit south of east, which was bad, and the current was strong, so it took about six hours. When I got to Charlestown, I picked up a mooring buoy, had some food and went to bed again. The next morning I did go to immigration. First, I had to go to customs, then immigration and then the port authority. It ended up being quite expensive and cost me fifty dollars altogether.

Nevis was lovely. Charlestown was a really pretty little town. I anchored off Pinney's Beach right under Nevis Peak, a huge volcano, which meant I had a bit of a lie in as it took the sun longer to rise over the mountain. I was also near the Four Seasons Hotel that had beautiful swimming pools just off the beach, and Jacuzzis, restaurants and bars. I wandered in and couldn't resist the Jacuzzi – a nice way to recover from two long days of sailing. I thought about spending another day relaxing there, but the next day hotel security were less welcoming. Although it was possible to buy a day pass for a hundred dollars, I decided to head for Guadeloupe instead. My plan was to stop off at Montserrat for a night on the way. I wanted to catch up with *Tara* and *Honey Ryder* if I could and be in St Lucia in time to meet my big sister, Jane, who was arriving in three weeks and would stay on *Sonic Boom* for a while.

I left Nevis early morning and made the thirty-five miles to Montserrat in about eight hours. I arrived after four o'clock (when customs closed) and left before they opened, so saved some money and paperwork again. The Soufriere Hills volcano that dominates the small island is still active so I sailed down the windward side to avoid getting covered in ash. It took me another eight hours or so to get to Guadeloupe.

Guadeloupe was amazing. Deshailes Bay was absolutely beautiful. Deshailes is where they film the TV series *Death in Paradise.* The day after I arrived, I swam with three dolphins, including a baby, less than twenty feet from my boat. I didn't try to touch them, but snorkelled above them in about ten feet of water. There were French restaurants lining the waterfront, I had a good meal and wine at L'Amer the day I arrived. There was a good French bakery as well. Everything was very French. Sunday morning was Palm Sunday and I saw lots of local people, all wearing red and white clothes, coming out of the very pretty church waving green branches.

I soon left Guadeloupe and headed to Dominica, a very different island. Much less French and much more Caribbean. They had the best national flag – a parrot surrounded by stars. I arrived in Prince Rupert Bay, a large sheltered bay in the north of the island. It was easy to anchor, and be near a good dinghy dock. There were wooden shacks on the beach, and bars full of Rastas and blasting reggae music out across the bay. It was a much poorer island and so much cheaper. Customs was only three bucks. There was a small town where I got some food and managed to get some laundry done.

Dominica was really all about the rainforest. There was lots of hiking, cheap up river tours, hot springs and jazz in the jungle parties. In a dinghy I went up Indian River, which flows into Prince Rupert Bay and saw where they filmed Calypso's house in the film *Pirates of the Caribbean.* Heading south along the coast to the capital Roseau I saw more dolphins and grapefruit. My friend Eddy, one of the pirates in St Martin who was from Dominica had said,

'You'll know you're in Dominica when you see grapefruit floating by.'

There was no wind so I had to motor most of the way. As I was approaching the bay, Desmond from *SeaCat* dinghied up to me, came alongside and sold me on a mooring ball. He helped me tie up for the night which cost ten dollars, but I didn't really have much choice. The shore drops off very steeply, so even close in it was too deep to anchor easily. It was the first mooring ball I had ever paid for. Once I was secure, I went to the Anchorage Hotel for a swim, shower, some food and water.

The next day I had a crazy sail to Martinique. I started motor sailing in the rain for the first two hours and had no wind until I was halfway there. I got to wear my foul weather gear for the first time. I was only doing about three knots and thinking it'd take all day. I made a cup of tea and had a cheese sandwich. Then came huge wind, and I went seven knots the rest of the way with my toe rails in the water. I got caught in a rainsquall, hit eight knots and got very wet, and then there were rainbows everywhere. I anchored in Saint Pierre for the night, but didn't go ashore, then went to Grande Anse d'Arlet the next morning but everything was closed, so I couldn't clear in or out of customs. The next day I carried on to St Lucia anyway.

I had another crazy sail at top speeds in strong winds to St Lucia. I dodged a few rainsqualls but got hit by one just off Rodney Bay. There were big waves so I had a really bouncy ride. Inside *Sonic Boom* was like a washing machine. I had put some tomatoes in a string hammock – it was a good way to store them, but I could see them smash against the bulkhead as the hammock swung violently from side to side. I couldn't leave the cockpit so ended up with quite a mess. There were a few other sailboats on passage, and it looked like everyone else was reefed, but I kept all my sails up and hung on for the ride. I arrived in Rodney Bay in record time, and I had made it just in time; my sister was due to arrive the next day.

I went to the airport, which was on the southern tip of the island to pick up my sister. The drive took us across pretty much the whole island. Through banana plantations, along narrow coastal roads, through small villages and Castries the main city. We got to the marina, jumped in my dinghy and motored back to *Sonic Boom*. *Tara* was there and we all went out for Chinese food.

We went souvenir shopping in Castries and explored Pigeon Island. On the beach, a Rasta was cutting open fresh coconuts with a machete, adding a shot of rum and selling them. We bought a couple and walked along the beach and into the Sandals Resort. At Sandals, they were in the middle of a photo-shoot for next year's catalogue. Possibly, my sister and I are visible in in the background of one of the shots, being asked to leave by hotel security.

Later, we sailed to Marigot Bay, a beautiful marina set in a natural mangrove lagoon. As we anchored, a local guy came out in his boat to welcome us and offer us anything we might like to buy. He introduced himself as Bushman (he mainly sold bush) and sang us a song about mosquitoes and how they tormented him. He was a funny guy and we ended up being good friends. I would bump into him again each time I anchored in Marigot Bay.

Behind the bay, through a narrow channel, there was an inner lagoon surrounded by mangroves. Here, there were lots of waterfront restaurants and bars and a very nice hotel with a beautiful swimming pool that had its own waterfall. We had rum cocktails and pizza in Doolittle's (named after the movie, which they filmed there). On my sister's last night, we went to The Rainforest Hideaway for drinks and live jazz: Emerson and the Empress; a beautiful Caribbean girl sang Amy Winehouse's *Back to Black*.

I spent a few weeks enjoying St Lucia. One day, I took a bus to Diamond waterfall and hot springs, which were fantastic. Swimming in a waterfall in the middle of a jungle is one of my favourite things to do. I went to Soufriere, a very pretty town with brightly painted wooden buildings and fantastic views of The Pitons, one of St Lucia's most famous landmarks. It was like taking a step back in time. With *Tara* I went for a sail, down the island from Marigot Bay and we all spent a night in Anse Chastenet, a beautiful beach in the south. Mark's son, Austin, came aboard as crew for the day so it was very relaxing for me.

I went to the Gros Islet jump up. Jump ups are wild street parties – loud music and dancing, mainly twerking (or doggy-style dancing as I've heard it explained). In Gros Islet, barbecues and bars lined one street, which had a stage with live music at the end. There was a parade with dancers, moko jumbies – stilt walkers, which represent ghosts and fire breathers. There were also weird dancing monsters – wearing masks. There was a man dressed as a pregnant woman and two rag doll people were on small platforms. It was like a scene from the film *Live and Let Die*.

I had been living on *Sonic Boom* for six months and had visited twelve islands since I set off from Tortola. So I celebrated with *Amaris* and *Honey Ryder* who were both now anchored in Rodney bay. We all met on *Amaris* for drinks, Sabrina awarded me with a torch for being the leading light and getting to St. Lucia first, even though I set off after everyone else.

The St Lucia Jazz Festival was due to start so we all moved our boats and anchored off Pigeon Island, very near the stage. We listened to the jazz coming from the main stage, and the sound checks, which were my favourite part. All the musicians had some stage time during the day to set up. I heard an awesome jazz version of Rihanna's *Diamonds* with only violins. On Sunday, the Commodores headlined. Pigeon Island had some good hikes up the hill with amazing views. There was also a beautiful beach where the Sandals Resort is and a nice old café with a book swap and a little art gallery.

After the Jazz festival, I went back to Martinique to pick up Steven from *Amaris*. He'd been in France for a week racing in the Outremer races, near Marseilles. So I checked out and sailed back to Grande Anse d'Arlet. I chose to spend the night there because it was so pretty and because there were free mooring balls funded by the EU. The next morning, I went to Fort de France, anchored and cleared in with customs – which was free. Everywhere should be like Martinique. I met Steven and the next morning, after lots of supermarket shopping, we headed back to St Lucia, and to *Amaris* which was still anchored in Marigot Bay.

We got hit by a rainsquall almost immediately, heeled over thirty degrees and were doing eight knots. After getting completely drenched, we soon got out of the rain and saw a huge whale breaching very close alongside. At first, I thought, *happy hello*, then I started thinking, *dangerous near miss*. The whale was probably as big as *Sonic Boom;* I don't think either of us would have done well in a collision. However, we passed each other safely and the whale went on its way. It was great fun sailing with Steven, we raced across the sea, getting up to eight knots, and it took us just seven hours to get to Marigot Bay. As we approached, dozens of dolphins swam alongside and played in *Sonic Boom*'s bow wave.

One evening, I had drinks and dinner on *Trinity*, who were there for a few days, trying to decide where to haul out for the hurricane season. It was so fun to catch up and hang out with them again. Robert and I had an amazing night out at the jump up and got very drunk. We'd stayed past the witching hour even though we'd been warned not to. Suddenly, it was two thirty, and we were getting into all kinds of trouble. Three times I think Robert saved us, mainly me, from twerkers, twerkers' boyfriends and some fishermen. I was laughing so hard I could barely speak so wasn't much help. Robert and Kerstin came aboard *Sonic Boom* and met my little sister, Sally and her boyfriend who were in St Lucia for a holiday. The meal was not so good but no one noticed after the painkillers I made, and we had another fun night. *Trinity* decided to haul out in Trinidad and soon left for Grenada. I was determined to get to Grenada before they left, and if possible, sail with them to Trinidad.

Rodney Bay and Marigot Bay were my favourite places in St Lucia. In Rodney Bay, I liked the fruit and vegetable boat that potted around the anchorage selling fruit. It was a very rickety old boat with a very rickety old man inside hidden by huge piles of fruit and veges that covered his boat. I liked the jump ups on Fridays and the pool and showers in the marina, although it was long dinghy rides everywhere. In Marigot Bay, I liked the waterfront bars, and free showers and short dinghy rides to everywhere, although the cafés and restaurants and mini mart were a bit more expensive. Motoring back to *Sonic Boom* at night all the lights from the houses built up the hillside would twinkle in the blackness as trees and plants briefly blocked them from view. It was a really magical sight and a magical place.

I took my sister and her boyfriend to Marigot Bay and we met up with *Honey Ryder*. For their first overnight on *Sonic Boom* I cooked a coconut curry, then we went and had drinks on *Honey Ryder*, and then we all went to the Rainforest Hideaway for live jazz. It was lots of fun, but when we got back to *Sonic Boom,* we'd been robbed. Cameras, phones, all my boxer shorts, my milk and a pineapple were stolen. We were all a bit shocked and sad. For me, losing my camera was the worst thing. It wasn't such a great one, but it had been given to me by Soni Park and so meant the world to me, and it took really nice photos.

We went to the local police station to report it and spent hours answering questions and making statements. The marine police offered to come to the boat to take fingerprints, but then they asked if I could take them in my dinghy.

'Better to take your boat,' I said, mainly because we wouldn't all fit in my dinghy.

'No man, da police boat been stolen.'

So the police didn't really fill me with much confidence. Instead we met up with Tom and Sabrina and our friend Archie and went to the St Lucia rum factory. It was a fun tour, followed by lots of tasting. I also managed to buy some cheap new clothes in Castries on the way back and felt much better. Although it would be another two weeks before I would find new boxer shorts.

I left from Rodney Bay, which was all the way at the north of St Lucia, so I had to sail for ten hours to get to St Vincent, my next stop. I decided to spend a night in Wallilabou Bay. What a magical place! I could see why Disney chose it as a location for *Pirates of the Caribbean*, and there were still some of the set buildings there, which, for me, added to the magic. There were props too – canons, a gallows and lots of coffins. I walked to a beautiful waterfall nearby, had a swim and washed off all the salt.

The next day, I sailed to Bequia and anchored in Admiralty Bay. Another amazing place, one that is very popular with sailors. Many cruisers spend most of their time in Bequia but I wanted to get to Grenada for the World Cup and to catch up with friends, so I only stayed for two nights. I then had a smooth sail to Carriacou where I'd heard there was an outbreak of Chikungunya (a disease from mosquitos). I stayed in Hillsborough Bay for a night and then headed to Grenada. I arrived in Grenada and anchored alongside *Trinity*. I felt like I'd made it – escaped to south of the hurricane belt. We both sailed round to Prickly Bay and met up with *Honey Rider*. We were all planning to head to Trinidad in a week or so.

Chapter 4
Trinidad

Grenada to Trinidad is an overnight passage. I was going to buddy boat with *Honey Rider*, which made it easier and more fun for me. We decided to leave Prickly Bay at ten o'clock in the evening and hopefully arrive the next day before customs and immigration closed. That way we would minimise the time spent in the dark. I had never set off in the dark before but managed to get my anchor up and motor into the channel without hitting anything. Tom and Sabrina had some issues but we were both under sail and heading out to sea by midnight.

At first we were close, sailing side-by-side, perhaps too close so we spread out a bit. I was worried they would soon disappear but I managed to keep them in sight the whole passage, which really made a difference – I could just follow their light, until I overtook them by mistake. We spoke on the radio every few hours, which kept me awake and my spirits up. Tom and Sabrina would take turns to do a four-hour watch while the other slept, and I was trying to stay awake until we got to Chaguaramas, our destination in Trinidad.

Trinidad is a big oil producer, has oilrigs way out to sea and lots of oil tanker traffic. A few hours into the passage, Sabrina radioed me to say she had spotted tankers ahead. She'd hailed one that was heading towards us on the VHF and let them know where we were going. I was very glad for the heads up. For a while I'd altered course toward a slow-moving cruise ship, until I realised it was an oilrig. Then I corrected course to head between two oil tankers.

'Tom, can you confirm the position of those two tankers, I'm good to go between them right?'

'Paul, that's a negative. Repeat do not head between. That's one tanker with a light at each end. Over.'

'Copy that. Will head behind it. Thanks, Tom. Over.'

With night sails I usually find the two hours before dawn are the hardest. The sunrise is always a beautiful and welcoming thing and brings with it a strong sense of having made it through the night. Coffee and a fried egg sandwich also cheered me up. A good morning call from *Honey Ryder* was also a boost. Later, we both noticed the turquoise blue Caribbean turn a cloudy green. We found out that it was due to the massive run off from the Orinoco River. We also both noticed a rise in temperature as we approached Trinidad. We were now only a few miles off the coast of Venezuela. Another few hours and we could see the cliffs of the mainland and the three islands just off it. We had decided to go through the first of the channels, Bocas del Dragón. Although it was the narrowest, and therefore subject to the strongest current, it was the closest which meant the shortest route to Chaguaramas.

Honey Ryder was a couple of miles ahead of me but looked to be headed to the second channel. I radioed Tom.

'Tom, are you sure that narrow inlet isn't actually the first channel?'

'Negative.'

'That fishing boat looks like it's headed that way.'

Then in the distance we saw a boat disappear through what looked like a small inlet in the rock face, and then another emerge from it. Soon it was obvious that it was the first boca and the way we needed to go. I carried on toward it, *Honey Ryder* altered course and we went through together. Once through, it was an hour's motoring to the anchorage. We slowly made our way past the steep cliffs and could see beautiful islands covered in thick jungle, and huge birds circling overhead. Then we passed navy and coastguard marinas and huge commercial boatyards with tankers and ferries hauled out of the water. Next we passed fishing trawlers and eventually came to where all the sailing boats were. Hundreds and hundreds of them.

It had taken us sixteen hours. We arrived just fifteen minutes before customs and immigration closed at four o'clock. We tied up on their dock and rushed in to complete all the paperwork. *Honey* Ryder then moved into Coral Cove Marina and I went to the anchorage, which was free. We found out later that the VHF channel we'd been using was the one used by Budget Marine, so we were being broadcast over their huge shop floor. We didn't know at the time, but all our conversations as we approached Trinidad had quite a big audience. It was a bit embarrassing, but we didn't care, at least everyone knew *Sonic Boom* and *Honey Ryder* had arrived in Chaguaramas.

I was anchored nicely in Chaguaramas Bay and met up with *Trinity* and *Nelly Rose* for more World Cup games and happy hour beers. Pim and Hanneke on *Nelly* Rose were an amazing Dutch couple on a round-the-world cruise. They had a relative living in Port of Spain, the capital of Trinidad, so after the Holland game we all spent the night at their nephew Fop's beautiful luxury apartment. It was the first night I spent on land since I moved aboard *Sonic Boom*. Solid floors (Chaguaramas was quite rolly) and walk-in showers, it was lovely. We all went on a trip to the Caroni Bird Sanctuary near Port of Spain with Pim and Hanneke and Liontien, Fop's fiancée. We motored slowly in a shallow-bottomed boat along rivers amongst the mangroves and saw snakes, iguanas and lots of scarlet ibises.

Trinidad is one of the cheapest islands. The street food stalls are incredibly cheap. There's a big Indian population, so there are great curries. My favourite was "doubles" – two egg pancakes with chana masala (chick pea curry), mango chutney and hot sauce. Only served early in the morning, and not my normal breakfast, but for four TT dollars (seventy-five cents), they were a bargain.

I managed to get work teaching English at a school in San Fernando and Tunapuna. I was teaching SAT exam classes, mainly essay writing to Trinidadian university undergraduates who were trying to transfer to a US university by doing well in the exam. One weekend, I managed a booth at the USA College Fair in the Hyatt Hotel Port of Spain. I got paid a few hundred bucks, got to try out the Hyatt's infinity pool, even got a supply of little bottles of shampoo. Life in Chaguaramas was very hot and humid; Sabrina and I wondered whether it was worth getting dried after a shower. I had free access to showers and Wi-Fi in the boat yards where *Honey Rider* and *Trinity* were staying. At Coral Cove marina, there was also a small swimming pool.

On a typical day, I would get up at sunrise, about six thirty, have a quick coffee and dinghy to shore. There I would have a shower, change into my work clothes and catch a maxi taxi to Port of Spain. From there I would get a shared taxi to San

Fernando, which took about forty minutes, once the cab was full and set off. From the taxi stand it was a short walk to the school. Sometimes I would take the big catamaran ferry from Port of Spain to San Fernando, and sometimes I would take the coach.

I was doing lots of traveling around Trinidad in cars, maxi taxis, catamaran ferries and air-conditioned buses. It was a busy, polluted stinky world – I missed white sandy beaches. Buses, or maxi taxis as they're called, cost five Trinidad dollars to get to Port of Spain, about twenty minutes away. POS is a big noisy polluted city but not without its charms, particularly the great colonial architecture. There were some amazing buildings; huge Victorian villas and public offices, as well as lots of little gingerbread houses.

The cicada that had been living under my cockpit table for the last two months was still chirping every night, keeping me company. I picked him up in Marigot Bay, St Lucia. For the first week, I thought it was a squeaky shackle, but then I figured out I had a new pet. Even though I knew what it was, I still couldn't work out where it was. Once, Kerstin came aboard and listened to the sound it made for ages and could not be convinced it was a cicada.

Out in the anchorage usually all the boats faced east, into the wind, but if there was no wind, a changing tide in Chaguaramas could make strange currents and all the boats would move around. I always think the boats look like they're dancing, as they swing round on their moorings in sync. On one day, we all did a full three sixty. The boats on either side of me were on mooring balls, but I was on my anchor, with a hundred and twenty feet of chain out, so I had a much bigger swing circle. We were slightly out of sync. As we all started to spin clockwise, I approached nine o'clock but the boat to my left was at three o'clock. Our sterns slowly headed towards each other, although I was sure we wouldn't hit.

'Hello, lovely day. Strange currents,' I shouted over.

Six inches, five, two, one, the other captain watched then suddenly disappeared to go turn on his engine. By the time he had, we'd passed, luckily overlapping at different heights so we didn't touch.

'OK, see you later,' I waved and headed off to three o'clock, and the boat to my right, which was rapidly approaching its nine o'clock. Had I anchored exactly between the two boats? I thought I was nearer to this boat, which would be bad. Again, we were going stern to stern and the other boat was looking very worried.

'Hi. How's things? Don't worry I'm sure we won't hit,' I said as I realised we were going to hit. The other captain disappeared and then reappeared clutching fenders. But we didn't. We missed by an inch. I relaxed, I was impressed with my anchoring, my neighbours not so much.

After three months in Trinidad, I renewed my visa. I had become part of the hard-core who stay with their boats over the hurricane season – mainly small, old yachts tied to beat-up dinghies with tiny outboards. Just like mine. I looked after *Honey Rider* while Tom and Sabrina go back to the states, and *Trinity* while Robert and Kerstin went back to Berlin. Twice a week, I checked their dehumidifier and batteries and cleaned the decks of bird poo.

During the summer, there was some bad weather in the Caribbean, but no hurricanes near Trinidad. A tropical wave did pass over one night and brought heavy rain and strong winds. There was flooding, trees down and landslides around the island. I rescued my neighbour's boat from another that had dragged on its anchor. I jumped in my dinghy to stop them banging into each other. Another windy day and a fishing trawler dragged and banged into me. I fended it off and fortunately wasn't badly damaged, just a bent rail.

At this time, there was lots of Chikungunya virus in the Caribbean, and it was getting worse in Trinidad. Sabrina on *Honey Rider* and their neighbours both got it, and it sounded pretty bad – a week of painful joints, fever, rashes. I was glad I was out anchored in the bay, where there were fewer mosquitos, but I still put a net over my hatch, a little clip-on, anti-mosquito fan in my cabin and citronella oil on the floor. I also regularly sprayed my feet and ankles.

As the hurricane season came to an end, Chaguaramas got busy, as lots of people returned to their boats and started getting ready to set off for another season of cruising in the Caribbean. Most people head to Grenada and then continue up the island chain, some go to the Virgin Islands. Tom and Sabrina also returned from their trip home to America, perfect timing for a customer appreciation party at Coral Cove Marina. I was happy to see them again, and *Honey Rider* was pretty much as they had left her.

For me, I was celebrating one year on-board *Sonic Boom*. More than twenty islands and hundreds of miles later, I was still afloat, and just as surprised as everyone else. An article I wrote about St Lucia was published in the November issue of *Sailing Today* magazine. I was on the dock with Tom when a sailor called out,

'Are you the sailor on *Sonic Boom*? I read your article in *Sailing Today*.' He had an online subscription so had read my article as soon as it came out. I got a pat on the back from Tom and had a smile on my face for the rest of the day.

Back down to earth, boat maintenance was taking over. In my free time I was sanding, painting and varnishing. I managed to get some free foam and cut it to fit my cockpit seat. Sabrina made a cushion cover out of some old fabric I had. And it transformed my life. Four-inch foam wrapped in Sunbrella, it was very comfy. My cockpit is over seven feet long and quite deep; it's a nice place to sleep. I wired up the solar panel Tom gave me, so I had solar as well as wind power and shouldn't need to use the engine, and, therefore, diesel to recharge my batteries anymore. I had problems with my head – every cruiser's worst nightmare. I thought maybe something had got stuck in a through hull, because my toilet wasn't flushing properly, so I jumped in (the bay) to unblock it. All the hoses were clear, so I took the pump apart. There was crap everywhere, literally, but I found the problem. I bought and fitted a new diaphragm and valves, cleaned everything and put it back together, and it worked. I found some teak oil sealer in one of my lockers and used it on my cockpit floor. I picked up some material with sailboats on the cruisers' net and made some more cushion covers. *Sonic Boom* was looking transformed from when I bought it a year ago.

In November, I hauled out at Peake's boatyard. It was very exciting to see *Sonic Boom* being lifted out of the water. Last time I cleaned the bottom, or tried to, I was chased off by thousands of little shrimp things that bite, two big crabs who were living happily on my rudder, and a kind of orange blob that popped out of what looked like a huge barnacle, and then sprouted yellow feelers. Once the boat was out of the water, but still next to the haul out slip, the hull was scraped and power washed. Then it was put on the back of a special truck, moved to my spot in the yard and put on chocks. I planned to paint the bottom of my boat with new antifouling. To haul out *Sonic Boom* cost three hundred dollars, which included five days on the hard. The paint was another six hundred dollars. There was a black market for cheaper anti-fouling; better commercial paint that fell off the back of a tanker, or from a friend of a friend who knows a captain that bought too much, but I decided to play it safe this time and paid over three hundred dollars per gallon for Sea Hawk.

The white stripe around my hull was peeling badly, so I scraped, sanded, primed and painted it, twice. I put on new letters, which my friend Chris, who has a stationary business, sent me from England. I cleaned my propeller with muriatic acid – a trick I learned in St Martin. Before I went back in the water, I smeared it with grease. Tom covered his with Sharpie magic marker ink, Pim put Propspeed on his, but that was very expensive, while *Trinity* put hot sauce on most things. I spent a few hours on my dinghy. I cleaned, lightly sanded, glued and pumped. I cleaned the old outboard and sold it for a hundred bucks. My dinghy situation was much better. Through some bartering and exchanging, with Tom's help, I managed to get a much nicer outboard engine for two crates of beer. It's a Johnson, like the one I had, but more powerful; up from three and a half horsepower to five. It was heavier to lift on and off the boat from the dinghy than my old one, so I made a harness and ran a line through the end of my boom so I could winch the engine up and swing it round into the cockpit.

After rough sanding and two coats of paint, I was ready and scheduled to go back in the water. *Sonic Boom*, surrounded by white boats, looked very blue. It was weird being out of the water; all the bounce had gone, everything on the boat became rock solid. It wasn't a nice feeling. It was a bit like running aground (although I didn't have much experience of that). Also, I felt very high up, and it was hot as hell.

Re-launch was problem free. Actually, I went in four hours early. Before breakfast, I launched my dinghy, attached the new outboard and went to pay my bill. All in all, for the haul and paint, the total cost was twelve hundred and fifty dollars; more than half of that was for the paint. I reckoned it was about twenty-five percent cheaper than it would have been in St Martin. In the States it would have been four or five thousand. When I motored out of Peake's dock, I noticed how much faster *Sonic Boom* was. The new paint and shiny propeller made a big difference. After going for a spin around the bay, I anchored back where I was before, then dinghied over to Crew's Inn for a swim, happy and exhausted.

I took the new outboard for a trial spin, I made some adjustments to the angle and by sitting as far forward as I could, I managed to plane for a while. Planing is when at full speed the dinghy rises up and then levels, with just the propeller in the water while the bottom skims along the surface. You need a fast dinghy and weight in the front to do it. While I was out of the water, I had tried to fix my dinghy, again; air was going out and water was coming in. I'd managed to fix the air leak but water was still coming in. I wasn't not sure I could fix it; the whole transom needed resealing, so my solution for the time being was to go fast and plane whenever possible to get water out.

Trinity came back, I was happy to see Robert and Kerstin again. They started getting busy preparing their boat to go back in the water. They were having problems and their teak deck was falling apart. The rubber seal that goes between the teak was rotten, so I helped them scrape it out and put in new sealer. I don't think anything could be worse than fixing my head, but that was pretty close. Robert and Kerstin ended up giving up the cruising life, sailing back to Germany and selling *Trinity*. Tom and Sabrina left a few days before me. It was sad to see *Honey Ryder* sail out of Chaguaramas, but I would meet up with them again.

One Sunday, Captain Kirk came aboard. Kirk from *Fiddler* came around with his German friend to see *Sonic Boom*. So I showed them round. The day before an old sailor had dinghied right up to me, waved and then slowly dinghied all the way round *Sonic Boom*. I wondered what he was doing. Finally he smiled and said in a thick American accent,

'Yup, sure is a pretty boat,' then left.

The next day I put out a call on the morning cruisers' net for a pilot book for Venezuela and Bonaire, and *Liberty* called back and said they had one. When I went to get it, the captain turned out to be the admirer in the dinghy.

I decided to leave Trinidad at the start of December and head to the ABC Islands. Sailing west would be very different from my sail south down the chain of islands. I would be faced with much longer sails for one thing and at least two overnight sails. One nice difference would be that the current and wind were behind me, which should mean fast easy sailing.

One problem I did have was pirates operating off the coast of Venezuela. A lot of cruisers even avoided Trinidad because it was so close to Venezuela, which has always been a risky place. Things had got much worse over the last couple of years. I had thought of stopping at Santa Maria but then I spoke to a girl whose friend was living on a boat there. She told me he was all right because he lived there but he'd said every boat that arrived got hit. I then thought about Los Testigos but was warned against going there as well.

'You must be crazy, that's where the pirates live. You'd be anchoring in their bay, they wouldn't even have to set off to rob you.'

I was starting to realise that everyone had a story, that most people advising me had never been there and none of them had actually ever met a pirate. Sabrina, who was very worried about me, introduced me to a captain who had met one. I found myself talking to a fellow cruiser who had a fresh scar down his forehead where he'd been hit by a pirate. Usually, his response to approaching pirates was to get his shotgun, go on deck and pump it so the pirates could see. Usually, this was enough deterrent, but on this occasion, he had fallen asleep and by the time he'd got his shotgun, the pirates were already on board. They grabbed the shotgun, aimed and pulled the trigger but he hadn't pumped it so nothing happened. The pirate reversed the gun and hit him in the head with the butt.

Most cruisers agreed it was best to stay at least forty miles off the coast of Venezuela. I also planned to avoid customs and immigration until I got to Bonaire. I'd heard that if Venezuelan customs stopped you, they would confiscate all alcohol and tobacco, and then notify pirates if they thought you had other valuables. I couldn't make it to Bonaire without stopping so I was going to make three stops on the way – La Blanquilla, Las

Roques and Las Aves. None of those islands have any kind of facilities. I may not even go ashore, so I needed to stock up on provisions in Trinidad. I was thinking it should take a week to get to Bonaire, a beautiful undeveloped island and a nice change from Trinidad. I'd stay there for a few days before going on to Curacao and Aruba. A few days before I left, there was a report out on the internet and on the news that the Dutch Coast Guard had given up patrolling around Curacao because they kept getting attacked by pirates.

I considered going back to Grenada, as a first stop to Blanquilla. Going to Grenada would mean I could buddy boat with *Honey Rider* and keep well away from the Venezuelan coast. In the end I decided to sail straight to La Blanquilla, about two hundred miles, but head north first to stay away from Venezuela. I hoped it would take about thirty hours.

My strategies for dealing with pirates were very limited. Dane always said the key is to not let them on board. Once they've boarded, you're in serious trouble. Going round and round in circles, I read, was a good way to make boarding difficult. I didn't have a flare gun but I did have smoke flares which I could try to throw into the pirate boat or even set off in my boat. I remembered a conversation on the cruisers' net in St Martin. One sailor had asked if wasp spray could be something to use. Another cruiser had replied and suggested bear spray would be better; wasp spray puts out a cloud of spray in front of you whereas bear spray is more directed and has a longer range.

I went to immigration and checked out. I was finally leaving Trinidad. Local radio had been playing non-stop "parang" – Christmas music, played by steel drum or "pan" bands. So to a calypso version of *Santa Claus is Coming to Town*, I pulled up my anchor and motored out of Chaguaramas. After over five months I was happy to be going and very happy with what I'd achieved there. *Sonic Boom* was massively improved with a new solar panel, a new outboard, new anti-fouling paint, and lots of wood, canvas and plumbing work done. I'd saved a few hundred dollars from teaching, I was clean, well-provisioned and excited about the long sail ahead.

Although I wouldn't miss Port of Spain or Tunapuna, some things I did miss about Trinidad – the great food and cheap prices. What I was missing at that moment though were white beaches, clear ocean and colourful fish. I was looking forward to chilling out in Los Roques for a while before heading to Bonaire, which was the next place for an internet connection. First up was an overnight sail through pirate-infested waters to La Blanquilla – I planned to leave at dawn.

Chapter 5
The ABC Islands

I left Trinidad early in the morning and was escorted past Scotland Bay by lots of very playful dolphins. They were jumping right out of the water and some of them were huge. I headed north to avoid pirates and was sailing fast. I was past Grenada by nightfall. Making good progress, I turned west and sailed well through the night.

Sailing at night is always a challenge, but often it can be very beautiful. When there's no moon and the sky and the sea are pitch black, the stars are amazing. I lie down and watch the sky as we move along. Looking out for passing ships, because the sea is black and the sky is too, it's sometimes difficult to make out the horizon. It leads to an incredible sensation of floating, not on water but on air. I discovered that lack of sleep leads to vivid hallucinations. I saw people, whales, other ships, islands…

The following day though, the wind completely died and I wasn't anywhere near La Blanquilla by nightfall. On the second night feeling completely exhausted, I hove-to for a few hours and got some sleep. I like heaving to; it's a good way to stop the boat so you can make a cup of tea, but I don't really like doing it at night. Trying to sleep while you're bobbing around in the open ocean in the dark is difficult. In the morning as the sun was coming up, I set off again toward La Blanquilla.

La Blanquilla turned out to be a really magical place. Firstly, it was almost impossible to see, invisible until I got right up to it. I thought I was going crazy, double-checking my charts and my GPS, which showed it to be only a mile or so away, but still couldn't see anything. Then I saw what looked like a very long wall about five feet high in the middle of the sea. It was black and completely smooth. It looked manmade. After two nights without sleep, I had started hallucinating, so I doubted what I was seeing, especially when it also appeared to be moving. I'd been sailing toward it, but after a while and without altering course, I was sailing alongside it. It seemed like something from the opening scene of Arthur C. Clark's book-based film *2001: A Space Odyssey*.

As I got nearer, I could see it wasn't a man-made wall, but a very smooth and tiny cliff face, maybe seven feet high. It was curved like a semi-circle, which explained why it had appeared to move from in front to alongside. I sailed along it for miles and miles and finally was able see the other side of the island, and an endless row of little coves and beautiful white beaches.

I still had an hour or two of sailing left before I reached the spot where I wanted to anchor, I stood up in the cockpit and stretched and yawned really loudly. Like a bear. I scanned the completely empty ocean and noticed a boat heading towards me. Did they think that my stretching arms in the air was a call for help?

'Guys, I'm just yawning,' I called out even though they were too far away to hear me. I was OK but realised by waving my arms and making hand gestures I would just be making things worse. Then I thought there was no way they could have turned toward me so quickly; they must have been heading my way before I yawned. In which case they were pirates. Perhaps they thought my yawning and waving was my fighting growl or something.

I still wasn't completely sure they were pirates. At least I didn't want to believe they were. I looked through my binoculars and could see their boat was an old fishing boat, painted pink and yellow, and I think named *Daisy Tom*. I thought that was a good sign. *Daisy Tom* sounded more like a children's clothing store than a pirate ship. This was just lots of friendly Venezuelan old men out fishing. I looked again through my binoculars, trying to keep them steady and in focus and I could see this time that they had three outboards. Three. Not one or two, but three, and they were big new looking ones. That was a bad sign, a very bad sign. There's no reason for a fishing boat to have three, they never have three. There's only one reason to have three – to outrun the coastguard. My top speed at that moment was about three miles an hour, maybe three and a half if I really pushed it. I looked at my jib; it was just hanging there lazily, loosely flapping. I started my engine. I was getting worried; they were headed straight toward me with a possible top speed of thirty miles an hour. Maybe much more.

This can't be happening, I thought and peered through my binoculars again. I guess I was hoping to see something else, or nothing at all, but this time I managed to focus on one of them standing on the bow. He was holding something above his head and shaking it. I adjusted the focus and tried to hold steady, straining to see. Then I gasped. I could see the man on the bow was holding a severed arm. A human arm, all pink and dripping with blood. I could see the hand hanging limply from the wrist, and at the end veins and sinews coming out of the elbow where it had been cut. Probably with a machete. He was grinning and shaking it madly, and their boat was still heading toward me, fast.

I was determined to not just give in without a fight. I must not let them on board, but I was helpless really. I started to realise this was going to end badly and probably very painfully. As their boat came even nearer this time, I could see that it wasn't a severed arm, it was a lobster and they wanted to know if I wanted to buy it.

'*Hola, amigo, langoster*?'

I shouted "*hola*", then shook my head, and off they went. Lucky for them, I was just about to let off all my smoke flares and start going round and round in circles. *What would they have made of that*, I wonder?

I continued making my way slowly along the beautiful coves and beaches. The water was crystal clear; I couldn't wait to jump in. I picked a very pretty cove with a palm tree on the beach, anchored very close to shore and went for a swim. My stay on La Blanquilla was like a very exclusive beach holiday or being a castaway on a desert island. There were no buildings, no other boats (once the pirates had gone), no people. Just me. I stayed for a few nights but could have stayed forever. It was exactly what I needed after Trinidad. In the end, water was the deciding factor. I was running low and needed to carry on.

Not all was well though. While I was anchoring, I'd noticed that my depth gauge was broken. I checked the transducer, and the monitor, and finally, found that some of the cable between the two had chaffed and partly worn through. It should be an easy fix once I got to Bonaire. Also, I had tangled my main sail halyard around my radar reflector and had to pull it tight, so that now I would have to go up the mast to get it back down. However, since the wind was directly behind me, I was sailing jib only, so I was happy to leave it up there for the time being.

I set off early morning for Los Roques. From La Blanquilla it was another overnight sail, about one hundred and twenty miles. The wind was very light so again it took longer than expected to get there. I was approaching the northern entrance through the outer reef at about four o'clock. Really too late to get to Sarqui, but I didn't want to spend a night hove-to so I decided to chance it and head in anyway. I needed good light to be able to see the seabed and coral and judge the depth. In lots of places it was four feet, and in some areas the coral rose up to within a couple of feet of the surface. *Sonic Boom*'s draft was nearly five feet so I had to be very careful. The light was fading, and a rainstorm was approaching, which was making it difficult to see the bottom, and my depth gauge (a crucial instrument in Los Roques) wasn't working. I wasn't having much luck.

At the last minute, I decided to change plan and head down the North East channel and round into Francisqui Lagoon, the nearest one. I kept my jib out until the last minute because I was running out of time, but when I did try to roll it up, it wouldn't move. My furlex was jammed, and the wind was picking up. I turned into the lagoon too early, bumped coral, and the boat jolted to a sudden halt. Crap. Quickly I reversed and pulled back, phew, but then hit coral again, this time with my rudder. It was like being trapped in a game of pinball. Then two Venezuelan guys, Pedro and Enrique appeared in their dinghy. They'd seen me from their boat – probably thinking, *Who's this idiot coming in under sail?*

'Put down sail, 'eez good idea, no?' they asked.

They helped me navigate into the lagoon and I dropped anchor at quarter to six, just as the sun was setting. I immediately tried to get my jib down.

I wrapped the jib around itself to stop it flapping, but the wind was really picking up and the stress on the sail meant I couldn't get it down. Then Pedro and Enrique appeared again in their dinghy. Pedro came aboard. I explained to Enrique as best as I could that the halyard goes up, sail comes down, and then went to the bow and pulled on the jib with Pedro. It would not budge. Now it was dark and really blowing. So I gave up, tied up the jib as best I could and left it, still flapping a bit.

Going back to the cockpit I noticed that Enrique was in his dinghy clinging for dear life to the jib halyard. Basically, Pedro and I had been pulling against Enrique, like a tug of war. I didn't try to explain to Enrique, who didn't speak any English.

'Oh, Enrique, you can let go of that now, thanks.'

Basically, we'd been playing tug of war with Enrique. I thought it would have been funny to have seen Enrique go flying up the mast as the jib came down, but as it was, it was just very frustrating. It was a stupid mistake caused by exhaustion. I got up before dawn and pulled it down by myself, but by then the damage was done – rips and tares. I was afraid it was going to be an expensive repair. For now I would have to go to Bonaire under main only. Once I'd retrieved my main sail halyard.

Los Roques was an amazing place. There was a huge ring of reef, miles across that created a massive lagoon, in which there were dozens of tiny islands, and more rings of reef making more, smaller lagoons. The wind was still strong, but the sea was calm, sheltered by the outer reef, making perfect conditions for sailing. The water was such a bright turquoise that its reflection turned the clouds green. It was an incredibly beautiful sight.

I spent a couple of days relaxing in the lagoon. I managed to make friends with another captain, Carlos, and he offered to winch me up my mast. So up I went, it took a while, and he was exhausted by the time a got to the top. By then I'd already realised I'd forgotten to release the clutch for the halyard, which therefore didn't move when I grabbed it. There was just no way to explain to Carlos from the top of the mast, so I signalled and he winched me down. He was pissed off – I don't think he thought it would be so hard. I didn't explain my mistake and how it'd been a complete waste of time. I also didn't ask him if he could winch me up a second time.

'Sorry, Carlos, thank you so much. Here, have a beer.'

The next day, I waved at a couple of Spanish cruisers as they passed me in the lagoon. They later dinghied over and were very interested in where I'd been and where I was going. So we had a good chat, and they helped me go up the mast, again. This time I got the halyard, but I'm sure Carlos saw and thought I was some kind of mad man who goes round getting people to winch me up masts. Even though I was singlehanded, there were times I absolutely needed help. Luckily, there's usually been someone there to help. It's always very touching when strangers are willing to help me. Human kindness is an amazing thing.

It was so beautiful; I would have loved to spend a few weeks visiting all the lagoons, anchoring off my own tiny desert islands. A real paradise fantasy, but one that would be brought quickly back to reality with a visit from the coast guard, or running out of food and water. I decided to get going to Bonaire. Leaving Los Roques I planned to avoid another overnight sail and stop for a night at Aves Barlovento, about fifty-five miles away; just about half way to Bonaire. So I set off early one morning and headed to Aves Barlovento. Pedro had told me to avoid Aves Sotavento, the neighbouring island, because there were coast guards there. I felt I was making progress.

Once El Gran Roques disappeared out of view behind me, the sea really picked up. The wind was good, nothing too strong, but the waves were huge. A massive swell from a distant storm maybe. I had the waves to my stern and my main sail fully out, so I was going fast up and down the waves. As the waves got bigger, I was going really high up and surfing down, I hit twelve knots according to my GPS (the theoretical top speed for my boat is seven). This was too fast and really I needed to put out a long length of warp or a sea anchor but didn't have either.

One big wave lifted and twisted me at the crest and I jibed – the boom swung all the way across to the opposite side of the boat at break neck speed (but maybe not Mach 1), with a massive swoosh, crack and then a sickening rip sound. My main sail had torn all the way across the bottom and was now in two pieces. The mainsheet track was smashed; trucks and shackles flew away like shrapnel. I jibed again and managed to grab hold of the main sheet as it flew by unattached, so I could pull the boom in. I tied the main sheet off on a cleat and used the jib winch, which luckily wasn't being used, to haul it in. I saw that the rip was just below the first reef line, so I put a reef in, and the sail was good. I carried on, a bit in shock.

Another big wave and another nasty cracking, splintering sound followed. I looked round and saw my flag, still on the pole flying away, below it I saw my outboard splash into the sea. The engine mount had split. *Quick, jump in? Turn the boat round?*

There was no point doing either, I just watched my outboard sink beneath the surface and to the depths below, lost forever. I sailed on, swearing as loud as I could for the next half hour. Then I just felt really sad and then stupid for not having secured the engine properly. It was absolutely my fault. Even though it only cost two crates of beer, I thought of all the trouble I'd had getting it and then servicing it, and how much it would probably be to replace it. Life without an outboard sucks.

I was tempted to make another overnight sail straight to Bonaire, but as I approached Aves, I decided against it and headed into another magnificent lagoon of dark blue and turquoise water. Again, I was cutting it fine, I dropped the anchor at six o'clock, and already the sun had gone. I ate, slept and set off at dawn to Bonaire, about ten hours away. Since leaving Trinidad, I'd covered over four hundred miles. I'd spent much longer doing those miles than I'd planned and unknown to me Sabrina was very worried. In fact, she'd contacted her friends on *Somewhere*, a boat I also knew from St Martin, to see if they had seen *Sonic Boom*.

'Sabrina, we're moored in the anchorage in Bonaire but we haven't seen him.'

'Please keep a look out, he's a week overdue and we're worried he got into trouble.'

'Wait a minute, there's a pale blue boat motoring into the anchorage now. It's *Sonic Boom*, and looks like he has had some trouble. We'll go and give him a hand.'

I arrived in Bonaire, just as the sun was setting, with all my sails ripped and hanging off. *Somewhere* helped me grab a mooring ball. Bonaire is a very popular scuba diving destination so there was no anchoring aloud to protect the coral. I went for Christmas Eve beers with *Somewhere* and another boat *Cheers*. We had dinner, and they all made me feel much better. The anchorage at Kralendijk was really beautiful. There was crystal clear water and great snorkelling off the back of the boat. There was a nice breeze, and I was even picking up free Wi-Fi from the shore. There were lots of cool bars and cafes with a strong Dutch/European feel. I missed my outboard, but I was near enough to shore so rowing wasn't too bad and I hitched dinghy rides whenever I could. Fireworks seemed to be going off on normal days, so New Year's Eve was especially spectacular.

There were some very strong winds that week, so I decided to stay in Bonaire a little longer. Really I was still recovering from the passage from Trinidad. I took my propane tank to the marina to be filled, which was expensive and took ages. I also filled up with water when I went to collect it. I was in slightly better shape to head to Curacao. There wasn't much in the way of chandleries or boat yards on Bonaire. I realised Curacao would be better for repairs, and I had lots. I needed major repairs to both sails, my depth gauge, and my bilge pump had died, with a little pop and a puff of smoke. Most of all, I needed a new outboard. I'd been rowing to a small beach to go ashore, but today a kid there managed to break one of my oars. That meant both sails, one engine and an oar were broken. I only had one engine and one oar left.

Thirty knot winds, gusting at over forty knots, were forecast for the whole week, which I don't really fancy in my condition so I waited for some lighter winds. I loved it in Bonaire, but the ten dollars per day mooring fee was killing my budget. I started thinking about Tristan Jones, and how he always managed to get out of trouble. I remembered he wrote how his mast broke one time, which was much worse than my problem. He made it to shore and in the night cut down a telegraph pole and used that. Although I also remember in St Martin, Jock said it was all fake. He'd just spent his life in a bar collecting stories from real pirates – like Jock.

I took the minibus from Harbour Village Marina to the Van den Tweel supermarket to get groceries. Usually there are shuttles like this for cruisers – the bus drivers charge a lot and make good money. Here though it was free. The supermarket paid the driver. It should be like that everywhere. The supermarket was awesome, a clean, air-conditioned paradise, it was like being back in Europe. I went straight to the olives and sun-dried tomatoes counter, asked for a cocktail stick and started to sample all the different types of olives, while I watched a bunch of cruisers wander round the supermarket in a kind of daze. Partly because of all the amazing food – fresh fruit and veg, bread and pastries, coffee and chocolate from Holland, but mainly because all the labels were in Dutch so apart from the obvious, no one knew what anything was. After check out, I spoke to some other sailors.

'Did you get some good stuff?' I asked James and Patti from *La Aventura*.

'Yes, we think so, we'll find out later.'

I'd asked a member of staff for stroopwaffels, one of my favourite Dutch foods. Stroopwaffels are a kind of cookie, filled with caramel and big and round so that they fit on top of a mug of coffee like a lid. The hot coffee then says hot and the caramel inside the cookie melts. It was also one of the only Dutch words I knew, but the staff member was local and she didn't know what they were.

'It's a kind of cookie, big and round,' I explained. She tried to help and pointed to various things on the shelves.

'No, that's a cheese cracker.'

'No, those are Oreos.'

'Now you're just picking up round things.'

Eventually, I found them and bought a packet.

Despite the high winds and the state of my sails, there was a small weather window that I decided to take. I sailed the forty or so miles to Curacao with a reefed in main, because that was all I'd got really. In the morning, I saw a boat called *Ouma* reefing sail and looking ready to go. I asked if they were going to Curacao, and they were.

'I'll follow you,' I shouted, thinking this would make life much easier. However, twenty minutes later, I was racing past them and they were following me. A huge rainstorm was also behind me. I used its winds to keep ahead of it, and then headed south a bit to let it past. I got one or two sprinkles, but nothing much. *Ouma* though, disappeared behind a grey block of rain. I was doing about seven knots and managed to keep ahead all the way, but the whole time I could see this wall of rain a few hundred yards behind chasing me, so it was a fairly tense sail. *Ouma* on the other hand, looked like they got sucked in and spent most of their day getting rained on.

Arriving in Spanish Waters with my main sail in tatters felt a bit like the scene in *Pirates of the Caribbean*, where Captain Sparrow arrives at Port Royal, climbing his mast as his boat sinks, eventually casually stepping off onto the dock. My boat had no sails, and my dinghy only had one oar. I followed the directions I had to Kima Kalki Marina, which was a lovely marina. Small, very private, tucked away in Spanish Waters amongst the mangroves and run by Ron, an old Dutch guy. I had to go stern to the dock, European style. As I motored into the marina, I dropped an anchor, swung round and reversed in, although it didn't go quite as cool as that sounds. I put another anchor out and felt very secure. Mateo on *Galaxie*, who I'd met in Bonaire, was there, and another boat I recognised from Trinidad. Mateo was from San Remo; unusually, I was surrounded by Italian sailors.

There were gale force winds for the following week, so I was stuck in the marina for a while. I took my sails to be repaired. I took the free bus to the supermarket and bought lots of food. I also went to Budget Marine and bought boat supplies, but things quickly slowed down to Caribbean pace. I went to Mambo Beach, which had bright white sand next to translucent turquoise water and was absolutely stunning. After I went to Willemstad, which was full of traditional Dutch architecture but painted bright Caribbean colours. I loved it.

Curacao was fun. I met some very interesting people in the marina. One of my neighbours at Kima Kalki used to be guitarist with the Dutch band Golden Earing, who had a big hit with *Radar Love*. They toured with The Who in the 1970s. With the money he'd made, he'd bought a sailboat. He told me a story of how once while sailing across the Atlantic in his Contessa 32, he bumped into Tom McClean, who was rowing across on his pioneering solo voyage and gave him some water. Another of my neighbours was recovering from a recent accident at sea. It was a very sad story; he had got into trouble in very bad weather and his partner had gone up the mast and was injured. A tanker had come to their aid but couldn't winch them off their boat because of the risk of smashing them against its hull. By the time the coastguard arrived and she'd been taken to hospital, he had tragically lost his partner.

One day, I went with Harry, my new German friend off *Leonotis,* another very interesting character, to Santa Barbara, which had a beautiful beach and a swimming pool. We had a good swim and cold beers on the beach. He'd decided to go sailing single handed after being heartbroken over a lost fiancée. He told me how once he'd been so depressed, he'd sailed out to sea and opened all his seacocks. Water poured in, and the boat started sinking, but when the water reached his knees he had a sudden change of heart. He pumped out all the water and decided to go on living. We had fun together. Later, I would find out that he died just one year later.

Being in the marina turned in to a mini refit. I pumped out all my engine oil (very black, went everywhere), refilled with clean oil and put on a new filter. I topped up my batteries and cleaned the propeller. The engine started first time and sounded good. There were no leaks anywhere, but it really needed cleaning, rust treating and repainting. I replaced the block and tackle for my main sheet, fitted a new stove (I was stoked about that), replaced the zinc anode under the boat (after three attempts), put new depth markers on my anchor chain and made a new flagpole. In Budget Marine they were forty dollars – typically overpriced, so I bought a broom handle for two bucks and screwed on a couple of mini cleats. I still needed to fix my depth gauge, as reconnecting the cables hadn't worked. I needed to replace the transducer that goes through the hull. I'd cleaned and patched (again) my dinghy, but I still hadn't found an outboard.

The wind finally died down so I checked out of Curacao. I sailed to Santa Cruz bay for a night before sailing to Aruba. It was seventy miles, so would take over ten hours to get there. The anchorages in Aruba are tricky with lots of shoals and reefs. I set off very early so I could anchor with plenty of light. The sail to Aruba was fast but hard. Hands shredded and another hat lost (as usual), and I was still having problems with my furling jib – it kept jamming, and the line keeps getting tangled. I had to drop the sail, untangle the line and put it back up at sea in almost gale force winds. When I arrived in Aruba, Port Authority were a nightmare, even more incompetent and unfriendly than usual. They broke my stern light, said I could stay on their dock overnight, then came back later and made me go anchor in the dark.

To get to the customs dock, I sailed up to the entrance of the bay, dropped sail and motored through the channel into the bay. I followed the markers and headed toward the customs dock. To get there, I had to motor down a channel that usually would have been very wide, but that day there was a cruise ship docked and it filled most of the channel. As I slowly motored down the channel right up alongside the enormous ship, passengers came out onto their balconies to watch the seemingly tiny sailboat pass by. I looked up at them from the cockpit and waved my arms like I was the first boat across the line. They all waved back, it was another triumphant arrival.

There was crazy wind in Aruba. It was too far, too windy and the sea too rough for me to row to shore in my dinghy. I'd be blown out to sea. I didn't really fancy moving *Sonic Boom* either until the wind died down a bit, so I was stuck on board until it did. Time to let my hands heal. A new power inverter I'd bought worked a treat – I could recharge my MacBook Air whenever I wanted. In the evenings, I used it to watch movies, write my blog and surf the web if I could pick up a Wi-Fi connection. After a few days of being stuck on *Sonic Boom,* I decided to move to Bucuti, where there was a dock and a nice bar and café, even though high winds were forecast for another week. Getting there would be very tricky, along a very narrow unmarked channel by the side of the mangroves. Everyone I asked said don't go right in the middle of the channel.

'Keep a third to starboard.'

'Wait, what?'

After the first channel, there was an even narrower channel which zigzagged across the lagoon to the anchorage beyond the marina and the boatyard. It was all made harder by the still massive winds, which were gusting to thirty knots, a strong two knot current and little fluffy clouds, which when they passed their shadows made it impossible to see the bottom and made dark spots on the water that looked like reef.

On the way I had to pass right by the airport runway lights. It was a restricted area, somewhere sailboats weren't allowed to anchor because the airplanes passing over are just about to touch down and might clip a mast. I was struggling against the current and got to the lights just as a huge Boeing was coming in to land. It was incredibly close. I could smell the exhaust and feel the hot blast from its engines. I carried onwards and thought I could see where I was supposed to turn ninety degrees to port. I checked the coordinates on the GPS, which was showing the whole area as red and white lines, and a warning: unchartered waters, depths from zero to seven feet. According to the guide I wasn't there yet, but I could see markers, so I followed them anyway. I went carefully across the lagoon in a big S and managed not to go aground, although I would do later in my dinghy. I found a good spot and dropped anchor near the other boats. Once I was set, I took a bus into Oranjestad, which was a lovely town. There were lots of colourful buildings, souvenir shops and casinos and a beautiful marina. I went to Starbucks and relaxed.

After a long search, I bought a new outboard: a Yamaha five horsepower two stroke. I'd noticed a Dutch sailor on a catamaran anchored next to me had an extra outboard on his rail, so I asked him if he would consider selling. I guessed it was about ten years old, and according to the owner, well-maintained and had apparently been serviced about six months ago. It had a brand new propeller still in the box, as well as impellers and spark plugs. It cost me five hundred dollars. Actually, it cost me all the cash I had – four hundred and forty dollars, thirty Euros and twenty-five Curacao Florin. I was so happy to have an engine again, but it was way more than I wanted to spend. It wasn't as good as the Johnson I lost, and that had only cost two crates of beer. This cost ten times that, but it was the best I could do, and actually I was quite lucky to have been able to do that good. It hadn't even been for sale.

There were a few boats waiting for the winds to die down a bit before leaving Aruba. I kept meeting cruisers who were taking the usual route – along the coast of Columbia to Panama. I bumped into *Cheers* in Renaissance marina. I'd been anchored next to Keith and Ida in Bonaire. They had a lovely boat, smaller than *Sonic Boom*, but brand new – everything was immaculate. They were on their way to Columbia. I also made friends with Mick and Isabel on *Ondular*; a very cool couple from Australia and Ecuador, sailing a really nice Beneteau 37, an ex-charter boat they'd bought in Tortola. Isabel was a TV star in Ecuador. One day, they gave me a dinghy ride into town, and we went to Starbucks for some free Wi-Fi and checked the weather. I had thought of going on to Panama, lots of people seemed to be going there, but the sea west of Columbia is one of the worst in the world so I'd changed my plan. I'd always dreamed of going visiting Jamaica, so my new plan was to stay in Aruba for a while and then go to Jamaica. My sister was due to arrive in ten days, so I would pick her up in Oranjestad and then we'd sail over to the beaches on the west coast.

Lots of people asked me about life on board, especially what I ate. For a typical day anchored at Bucuti, I would wake up at seven, have a coffee and go for a swim (Usually, I just dove off the back of the boat). For breakfast I ate fruit salad – banana, pineapple and apple. For lunch I had something simple like a sandwich or cheese omelette with salad, and for diner, I often made pasta or a coconut curry with rice. I used to read *A Girl Called Jack*'s blog sometimes for recipe ideas. When I provision, I go to local markets whenever possible. In Willemstad, there was the floating market in Punda and fresh fruit and vegetables from Venezuela. There was a similar one in Bonaire – set up by Venezuelans who had sailed over to sell their farm produce. I got whatever was cheap and fresh. I tried not to chase after things I missed (usually expensive) and went local instead.

After breakfast, I motored over to Veradero marina, filled up with water and washed my decks down, which were still covered in salt after the passage from Curacao. After lunch I had another swim and went grocery shopping. In the afternoon, I took my outboard, which turned out to be a 2002 model, to the mechanic and put on the new propeller. That made a big difference – it was much faster, and felt a bit more like a five-hundred-dollar engine. It was leaking water – probably a corroded gasket or seal, but that wasn't urgent, and since it was very difficult to get the parts on Aruba, I decided to leave it until I got to Jamaica. After a shower at Bucuti Yacht Club, I went for a ride around the bay and managed to plane for a while. I had a swim before dinner, then I watched *The Life of Pi* (the strong wind meant I had lots of electricity) and went to bed around eleven o'clock.

I moved back to Renaissance Marina in Oranjestad because my sister Sally was due to arrive. The marina was part of the Renaissance Hotel complex, so we got to use their pools and beach and showers. We took the free boat taxi to Renaissance Island, where there were beautiful beaches, including one with flamingos. The wind died down a bit so we sailed from the marina to Hadicurari beach, on the west coast of Aruba. With just my jib we still averaged around seven knots, so it only took an hour or so. I'd serviced my furlex while I was in the marina and found that a screw had broken loose and jammed the mechanism. I cleaned, de-rusted and re-greased it and replaced the old furling line. It was working well again. For the next few days I'd had enough boat work. I'd decided I was going to be a beach bum for a while.

Getting close to shore on the west coast was very tricky because there were lots of unmarked shallows. I'd worked out a course and tried to stick to it very carefully. We anchored alongside two pirate ships, quite far from shore, but even there we were in only about eight feet of water. After anchoring, we launched the dinghy and went for a walk on the beach, had a swim and rum cocktails to celebrate a successful passage. Hadicurari and Palm Beach were absolutely beautiful with lovely white sand and clear turquoise water. Although it was very built up – there were huge Marriott, Ritz Carlton and Hyatt hotels, they were all beautifully landscaped with beachside pools and Jacuzzis and there was a lovely beach path than ran along most of the beach. All the hotels had slightly different beach towels so I started a collection. It seemed like most guests were American and some South American. It felt like we could be in Miami. I watched *Hot Bench* and *R U Faster Than a Redneck?* simultaneously on two TVs in Starbucks.

Chilling on Hadicurari beach was cool. There were showers all along the beach, but we also found inside ones. The Marriott had one of the nicest pools, but after getting busted at the Hyatt, our new favourite place was on the beach next to Moomba, which wasn't part of a hotel. There were cheap sun lounges and a nice bar with free Wi-Fi. There were also water and ice machines everywhere, and nice bars for happy hour beers watching the sunset. It would have been easy to stay for a long time, but after another few days we sailed to Boca Catalina, a small cove nearby great for snorkelling. Even though it wasn't very far, it was a tricky sail. Leaving Hadicurari we bumped the bottom and got stuck for a few minutes, which was quite scary. Underway, it was still so windy I put out a reefed main and we were still doing six knots. When we arrived, I had trouble setting the anchor because the bottom was just a thin layer of sand over rock, but the third time I managed to hit softer ground, and we anchored for the night.

The sail back to Oranjestad was a bit better. We were straight out into deep water, and we sped down the coast with a reefed main. On the way we got stopped and boarded by the coastguard, which was annoying. After they'd left us (unimpressed), we rounded the corner and were headed straight into the wind and waves. I kept the main up and motored, but still we were doing less than two knots and it took over an hour to get to the marina. We were happy to arrive, washed the boat, did laundry, had a swim and shower, and went out for dinner.

After another couple of days I said goodbye to Sally and was very sad to see her fly away, we'd a lot of fun. I moved from the marina, back to the airport anchorage just off Nikki Beach feeling a bit blue. Not helped by the fact my outboard needed repairing before I could use it again – the leak had become urgent. The Dutch guy I bought it off on *Jammin* wasn't very sympathetic.

I started getting ready for the sail to Jamaica. Paper charts and a new Garmin chip for the Southwest Caribbean would hopefully arrive soon, with new guests/crew – Paul and Ben. I went back to the marina to pick them up. The three of us would try and leave once we'd provisioned. It's a five hundred mile sail to Jamaica, so it would take at least three nights to get there.

I picked up Ben and Paul at the airport and took the straight to *Sonic Boom*, which was tied up in the beautiful marina in Oranjestad. They dropped off their stuff and we went out for food and beers. Unfortunately, they hadn't brought the Garmin chip, so my chart plotter wouldn't be much use, neither had they brought a paper chart. So we would be sailing blind. I felt like abandoning Jamaica and heading to the Dominican Republic instead – a much easier, shorter passage.

I had a day or two to try and get charts in Aruba. I tried, but failed. I double-checked the chart plotter but without the chip, I couldn't see Jamaica in any detail, just a small vague yellow square. Ben had already booked a hotel in Jamaica, and they both had flights booked out of Montego Bay so I decided to go anyway and be very careful as we approached the coast.

Passage Weather was showing big yellow blobs off Columbia, sometimes orange, instead of the usual pale blues. Windguru showed one big block of bright pink for the whole week, which meant winds gusting to thirty-five knots. Big seas were also forecast. We bumped into Keith from *Cheers*; they had decided to give up, go back to the US for a month and hope it would be better when they returned. *Ondular* will chance it and try to hug the coast. I was glad we were headed north, away from the storm.

Even sailing north it was going to be very windy for the first day and night at least, but at least we'd be sailing away from the worst of it and hopefully into calmer seas. We planned to leave at lunchtime on Monday. For Jamaica, Windguru was showing nice pale blue and light green, ten to fifteen knots and calm seas. I was hoping to arrive on Thursday. At least that was the plan.

·

Chapter 6
Jamaica

I set off from Aruba with Paul and Ben after lunch. First we had to motor over to customs and immigration and by the time we'd got through it was late afternoon. We motored out of the channel and put up the sails. As soon as we'd left the harbour, the wind and waves picked up and we started racing along under a reefed main and full jib. Ben spent the first day throwing up and the second day sleeping but then did all his watches really well. Once we accidently jibed as Ben was standing in the hatchway, the boom swung across just missing his head. It probably would have killed him had he been two inches further out of the hatch, or else knocked him overboard which probably would also have been fatal. As the traveller zipped to the other side of the cockpit, the mainsheet though grazed his knee – pretty badly.

The scariest moment happened when I was alone in the cockpit, while the others were sleeping. We were literally in the middle of the Caribbean Sea and the waves were really picking up. *Sonic Boom* surfed straight down a fifteen-foot wave and I saw the bow dip down into the water. I was looking straight down; *Sonic Boom* was almost vertical and I really thought we were going to pitchpole (flip end over end). I froze and took a big gulp of air. But at the last minute *Sonic Boom* came around through the wave and carried on surfing. I could feel the power of the boat slicing through the water, and the strain on the hull, the sails, everything. It was a really incredible moment and another time I'd been saved by the strength of the Elizabethan.

We were all exhausted mentally and losing concentration. None of us felt like eating really, and it was very difficult to even stand up in the cabin, let alone cook. But I knew we needed to eat properly. We'd bought lots of vegetables and rice for curries to eat under the stars in the cockpit with a few beers, but the wind and waves meant we were heeled over and bouncing around a lot. I cooked baked beans and fried potatoes, toasted egg and cheese sandwiches instead. One hand hanging on to the boat and one hand holding the bowl of food, a romantic evening dinner it was not. But the change in mood and energy levels was a welcome relief.

We'd had twenty-five to thirty knot winds all the way, so it took us ninety-six hours, averaging seven knots, but reaching eleven, even with the main sail reefed. We also had some very big seas. Waves were crashing over the deck and we were getting lots of water in the cockpit. After a big squall on the first night, Paul found a fish in his bed. After four days and four nights at sea we sailed through a little channel into Port Antonio, Jamaica.

Port Antonio was beautiful, a laidback coastal town with the spectacular Blue Mountains in the distance. There was calm water and not so much wind. We had beers and burgers on arrival to Errol Flynn Marina. It was named after the swashbuckling movie star who had lived in Port Antonio in the 1950s. It was very pirate – there were old cannons and huge old anchors dotted around the grounds. We pulled into a dock and cleared in with customs and immigration. Next we cleaned up the boat and did masses of very stinky laundry. After two days of putting the boat back together, filling up with water and provisions we decided to take a break and explore the island.

Paul and I went to Reach Waterfalls. A taxi took us through the countryside and into the mountains. We trekked through some jungle and arrived at a large calm pool. We jumped in and cooled off. There was a waterfall leading into another deep pool below us. We jumped into that pool and swam to the edge where there was another waterfall, leading into another slightly smaller pool. We did this five times, swimming through pools and jumping down waterfalls working our way back down the mountain where we met the taxi again and went back to Port Antonio. It was great to be swimming in freshwater and a nice change to be in the mountains surrounded by green instead of blue.

It seemed a shame to leave Port Antonio. Errol Flynn Marina was one of the nicest marinas I've stayed in, but I was excited to see more of Jamaica, so Paul and I set off from Port Antonio to Oracabessa, where Ian Fleming's house is. However, we were very delayed setting off and then the wind died, which meant we couldn't make it before dark. I didn't fancy a small cove, narrow channel and lots of reef in the dark without charts so we gave up on that plan and decided to sail on through the night.

We turned the engine on and kept going for a while, hoping for Discovery Bay by morning.

Around ten o'clock, we saw a lot of lightening, almost constant flashing in the distance, but getting closer and closer. Paul had a look of terror on his face. He later said that he'd never been so scared in his whole life. I'm often asked if I ever feel afraid out at sea alone unable to see land. I never feel afraid, I love it. There's a tremendous sense of freedom. You are alone with and at the mercy of nature. I've been through enough storms to know and be aware of the constant potential danger. Life should be intense. It's too easy to be satisfied with comfortable and not experience the wonders of the world.

Out at sea I have seen some of the most amazing things; watching huge black rain clouds with a wall of water beneath them as they empty into the sea and gradually disappear, or the reverse – huge water spouts being sucked up into a cloud. The sounds as well; so many times I've thought what is that noise, only to look around and see a wall of rain rapidly come towards me. I see the line it makes as it moves over the sea and then I'm in it getting drenched in a shower. However, having a forty-foot metal mast pointed to the sky, lightening is not my favourite thing.

We headed north a little and eventually managed to let the storm pass behind us. It was a close thing; we could see the wall of rain and felt a few drops. The very strong winds were making us tense, but we were now doing up to eight knots. We dodged a couple more very scary looking squalls and eventually made it to Montego Bay. Dolphins cheered us up after a rough night running away from lightening. There were a few playing in our bow wave. We anchored off the Royal Montego Bay Yacht Club, which was a real old colonial time-warp kind of place. We anchored and went ashore for burgers and beers, too exhausted to do anything else. It had been another hard sail.

I spent a very relaxing couple of days lounging by the pool at The Roundhill Hotel where Ben and Paul were staying before they flew back to London. The hotel was lovely with dark, polished wood villas set in beautiful tropical gardens. Everything was Ralph Lauren – furniture and fabrics, even staff uniforms. He actually had a house right next door, and apparently often visited.

Back on my own, I planned to stay in Jamaica for a few weeks and explore the island a bit more. I tuned in to Irie FM, listening to reggae in Jamaica gave me goose bumps. There was great music everywhere. The annual music festival in Montego Bay, the Red Stripe Reggae Sumfest, started while I was there. The stage was just across from where I was anchored, so I could hear all the bands.

I spent time visiting the beaches of Montego Bay and hanging out at the Yacht Club. The Yacht Club members got together on Friday evenings for food and drinks around the pool. As a visiting yacht, I was an honorary member, so I met some very interesting expats and sailors, who had been there for years. Irish, Canadian and English, there seemed to be a fairly tight-knit expat community in Jamaica. Just over the road from the Yacht Club was Sunset beach, which had a pool, restaurant and showers, and was available to Yacht Club members. It was my favourite beach to spend the day on.

I took a shared taxi from the Yacht Club to downtown Montego Bay for two hundred dollars (US two dollars), where there were a couple of really beautiful beaches in small coves, near Gloucester Avenue. This was also where the bars and clubs were – all night parties at Pier 1 and Magaritaville. It was quite touristy but fun to see the Jamaican Olympic bobsleigh, from the film *Cool Runnings*, in a bar on Gloucester Road. One evening Jack from the Yacht club took me to happy hour on the House Boat – a floating bar in Bogue Lagoon. There was a tiny little ferry, with a bell and a ferryman that took us from land to the boat, which was only about fifteen feet away. I noticed the boat listed to port slightly. It was because the smoking section was on the port side.

I was invited to go for a sail around Montego Bay in a thirty-foot trimaran called *Skedaddle*. It was a very fast boat – we did fifteen knots in only slight wind. I sailed with Peter, the owner, and some other people from the Yacht Club. We docked off Doctor's Cave Beach for late lunch and a swim. Doctor's Cave beach was one of the most famous beaches in Jamaica. The beautiful turquoise water off the white sand beach was once thought to have curative powers. There were showers on the beach and inside, as well as a nice bar and restaurant. It was also in a really nice part of town; a little touristy, but not as hectic as downtown. There were parks and pretty old buildings, cool bars and restaurants, as well as lots of souvenir shops. My neighbour Dana, on the catamaran *Vida Libre* came with us and we became good friends. She was going back to the states for a couple of weeks and I said I'd keep an eye on her boat for her.

Days seemed to float by in Montego Bay, just chilling on *Sonic Boom* watching the boats coming in and going out again. Charter catamarans, sailboats from the yacht club and every few days a cruise ship came in to dock. I went to the supermarket, had a swim in the pool after lunch and in the evening went for a beer with Dana. It was so nice there; showers, beaches, bars and shopping all nearby, all cheap, and also cool, I didn't want to leave.

I went to Negril to check it out. I swam in Bloody Bay and had lunch on Long Bay. Also known as Seven Mile Beach, it was a spectacular beach and very laid back, with Negril town at one end and Bloody Bay at the other. It wasn't seven miles long though. I bumped into my friend Abby, whom I'd met in Port Antonio, and it was lovely to see her again. It was my plan to make friends with Lilly Allen. She had a house in Jamaica, but I hadn't seen her yet. One weekend it was Emancipation Day and another it was Independence Day. Both meant public holidays and big parties everywhere. I helped Dana with a charter – a couple from New York wanted an afternoon sail around the bay and made a few bucks.

I started getting ready to leave Jamaica and preparing the boat – I fixed the compass light and the salon light broken during the passage from Aruba, cleaned up the engine a bit, topped up the oil and tightened two very loose belts. I also re-furled my jib so it was the right way round and cleaned the propeller. I checked out of Montego Bay and sailed to Negril. I anchored in Bloody Bay and had dinner. The water was so clear I could see hundreds of tiny transparent box jellyfish. The next day, I went snorkelling and saw lots of beautiful purple fan corals and squirrelfish. The Cayman Islands were two hundred miles away, so it would be a good overnight sail. My plan was to head to Cayman Brac first, and then after a few days, on to Little Cayman and finally Grand

Cayman. I just had to wait for a weather window. I hoped I would be able to come back to Jamaica soon.

Chapter 7
The Cayman Islands

The sail from Negril to Cayman Brac was one of my best ever. There was a flat sea and enough wind to go six knots – beautifully smooth gliding through the water. I had little birdies flying along with me, catching the air currents, darting in and out of my sails, trying to land on my spreaders and hitch a ride. Birds often come and fly between my sails. I watch them play, trying to surf the air currents. It makes me think the sails are essentially wings. I fly along, albeit moving left or right instead of up and down. A bit like a duck with one wing pointed up and one foot in the water.

That night here was no moon, the sky was black, and so was the ocean, making it difficult to see the horizon. This always gives me a strange sensation of floating in air rather than water. Sailing along watching the Milky Way pass overhead I saw dozens of shooting stars, one massive one that lasted a few seconds and had a sparkling tail. Shooting stars are actually meteors entering the earth's atmosphere, and these seemed so close I half expected to hear them splash down.

My new homemade autopilot worked like a charm. I barely touched the tiller the whole passage. I'd found a copy of John Lecher's rare book *Self-Steering for Sailing Craft* and borrowed it from Jack at the Yacht Club who didn't know he'd had a copy. I prepared everything I needed for sheet to tiller self-steering. From the tiller, on one side I had a line running through a block and across the cockpit to the main sheet, putting a bend in it so that when I sailed tension in the main sheet pulled the tiller. On the other side of the tiller were lengths of bungee that pulled the tiller back when there was less tension in the main sheet. Essentially changes in wind strength create a movement on the tiller that keeps the boat on course.

In the morning, the wind died and I had to motor the last twenty miles, which took four hours. The water around Cayman Brac was unbelievably blue and cheered me up. I arrived at Creek where I could check in. Immigration was easy. Three officials came on board *Sonic Boom* to check my papers and fill out paperwork. The guys were cool – one sprayed the boat for mosquitos, which cost thirty-one dollars, the others asked me questions.

'Do you have any secret lockers?' one of the officials asked.

'No,' I replied, thinking that was kind of a dumb question. The customs guy laughed.

'You'd be surprised how many people say yes and show us.'

He then asked me if I had any alcohol.

'I've got half a bottle of rum,' I said, and this time they all laughed.

'Ain't no worth botherin' 'bout no half bottle of rum.' They all laughed again.

After they left I turned the engine on, untied and left to pick up a ball a little further down the coast. Here there were free mooring balls everywhere – and shower blocks too. I went to bed thinking how nice it was to arrive after a passage and the boat still be in order. That didn't last long, I woke up in the middle of the night and saw everything being churned around like a washing machine. A very big storm was passing over Cayman Brac with huge winds and lots of lightening, I bounced around on the mooring ball and everything got thrown around inside. In the morning, I saw my dinghy paddle had blown away, and my wind generator had stopped working.

Each day I untied, sailed further along the coast and picked up a new mooring ball. At Scott's Anchorage, there was a bar and restaurant and a supermarket. I had beers and pizza at Barracudas Bar and bought some groceries. And some ice – it was incredibly hot. Getting to shore without an outboard was hard work, especially without oars. I made a paddle out of a broom handle and a flipper. Desperately, I needed an engine; I hoped I could get one on Grand Cayman.

Even in forty feet of water I could see the bottom off the back of my boat. Snorkelling was like swimming in an aquarium. Around the pier at Scott's Anchorage I saw parrotfish, a big stingray, some sergeant majors, and lots of little bright orange and blue fish, starfish and anemones. I decided I had to go diving. It was an opportunity I couldn't resist – scuba diving in the Caymans is some of the best in the world. I went on a dive to the wreck of the *Captain Keith Tibbetts* – a three hundred and thirty feet Russian frigate under sixty feet of water, and one of the best dives in the Caymans. It was amazing to see the ship, which was lying in two pieces. There was lots of sea life: coral, sponges, hogfish and a sea turtle. It was a fun dive, although a very strong current made it hard work, and I used my air quite quickly.

I went on another interesting expedition to Donald Crowhurst's forty-foot trimaran *The Teignmouth Electron* that lay on the beach near the airport. Crowhurst went mad in The Golden Globe, the 1968 race to circumnavigate the globe nonstop single-handed. He'd had problems with his boat right from the start and gave up the idea of a circumnavigation, but needed to finish or risk going bankrupt. He decided to make up his positions to make it look like he'd been all the way around. After sailing around the Atlantic and faking his log for a few weeks, his boat eventually started falling apart. It was later found adrift with a sail up, but Crowhurst's body wasn't on board and was never found. The boat was later bought, then abandoned on Cayman Brac. It was sad to see the boat as a wreck on a beach. I could sympathise with Crowhurst's state of mind.

I sailed from Cayman Brac to Little Cayman five miles away. Even smaller than Cayman Brac, only a hundred people lived there. I wanted to go to Owen Island, a tiny deserted island in South Hole Sound. It looked amazing, but it was too rough to enter the channel, so I picked up a ball in Bloody Bay further around the coast. I was above a reef shelf which was at about forty feet, but just behind me there was a vertical wall that dropped to the depths, thousands of feet below. It was absolutely stunning. It was a popular dive to go along the wall, but even just snorkelling was amazing; I made friends with another sea turtle and saw a big barracuda.

Meanwhile, tropical storm Danny, formed off the coast of Africa, was in the Atlantic, had turned into a hurricane and was headed my way. It might fizzle out, veer to the north, land on Dominica and miss the Caymans. Then again it might not. My hurricane plan was to head to Grand Cayman and Governor's Creek, North Sound, but from where I was that would be an overnight sail, after checking out with Cayman Brac immigration, so it wasn't much of a plan really.

I left Little Cayman and motor sailed backed to Cayman Brac and Scott's Anchorage. I went snorkelling over the sunken wreck *Kissimee*, which lay upside down just off the pier. I saw some stingrays and a turtle, dove down and swam right through a huge shoal of little bright blue fish. Little Cayman and Cayman Brac were both amazing. It was a really nice change to spend time on desolate islands and empty beaches again and also cool to spend time in the underwater world. Snorkelling and diving were fun; I was looking forward to doing some more on Grand Cayman. I checked out of Cayman Brac and was ready to sail to Grand Cayman. The wind was very light so I planned to spend another night on Little Cayman on the way, if it died completely. It was about ninety miles, which meant another overnight sail. I wanted to leave just before sunset and, hopefully, arrive in the morning.

The sail to Grand Cayman was an adventure. I went to clear customs and immigration, but two dead bodies had been found in a boat drifting off shore, so Scott's anchorage was taped off like a crime scene, as they towed the boat in to the dock and took off the bodies. Unfortunately I was trapped in, which meant I was delayed a couple of hours, so I stopped in Little Cayman one more night. The next day there was very little wind, so it took me two full days to sail the ninety miles. I didn't want to motor all the way, so on the first night I dropped the sails and went to bed. *Sonic Boom* just drifted in vaguely the right direction.

With so little wind, during the day it was incredibly hot. The deck was too hot to walk on. Inside was like an oven. Turning the fan on was like turning on a hair dryer. I could feel myself getting hotter and hotter. I kept having showers until my water ran out, then I pulled up buckets of seawater and tipped them over my head, but it only had a brief effect. At one point, I was sick and realised things were quite serious. I jumped off the boat to cool down – a very dangerous thing to do. The boat was still moving so I hung on tight to the rope ladder and, eventually, cooled down. In the afternoon, I saw loads of dolphins, which cheered me up. They stayed with me for an hour or so, jumping out of the water and blowing air.

Finally, I arrived in Grand Cayman. First I took a buoy by the channel entrance into North Sound and jumped in again to try and cool down. I called Port Security and asked if I could check in at the Yacht Club in Governor's Creek. They said yes so I went there. Immigration and Customs were annoyed. Really I should have gone to George Town, but they'd heard my talk with Port Security on the radio, so they weren't angry with me so much. A long narrow channel led into North Sound – a huge shallow lagoon in the middle of the island, with small channels to other lagoons and canals. I followed the buoys into the lagoon and headed to another channel that led to Governor's Creek.

I felt a lot more secure in Governor's Creek, where there was a lot more protection from wind and waves. The creek is actually a small man made lagoon ten feet deep surrounded by mangroves. There weren't many sailboats there, which was good, although that would change if a hurricane looked likely to hit. Danny fizzled out, but then there was Erica. Although the models were predicting a path north to Cuba, missing the Caymans, it was still a worry. My plan would be to wedge *Sonic Boom* as far as possible into the mangroves, drop both anchors and tie up with mooring lines, take everything down – sails, lines, dodger and hope I don't get hit by debris, or boats that had come loose.

I went ashore to do laundry and met a couple of old pirates living next door to the launderette in West Bay. One reminded me of Jock and told me old stories, how he got caught smuggling conch and lost his boat. The other was called Owen Evans – definitely a distant past Welsh connection. Afterwards I headed to Seven Mile beach, just a short walk from the Yacht Club, and one of the most beautiful beaches I've ever seen. I walked along the northern part and went for a swim. To the south were the big hotels and George Town.

I was anchored away from all the other sailboats in the Creek because I needed to be close to shore. I was actually near a popular fuel dock, and a few captains have called out to me while bunkering up. One old man motoring out of the creek on top of his old Boston Whaler shouted out, 'Nice boot man,' as he went past.

In the shop, someone else asked, 'Is that your little blue boat? Lovely.'

There was a real mixture of American and Caribbean cultures in Grand Cayman. There was North American: KFC, Burger King, Marriott Hotels, Ford pickups, and country and western music was huge. There were a lot of North Americans on holiday – diving and fishing; it's not so far from Florida. There were also a lot of Spanish speakers from Central America, Honduras in particular. I also met South Americans from Columbia. There were also strong links to Jamaica, and lots of Jamaicans lived there, they smiled and shouted hello if I was wearing my Jamaica T-shirt. Jamaican pasties were popular.

I tried to fix my wind generator; I looked at all the connections, the fuses on the regulator and the brushes inside. They were all fine, I did a few more checks but then faced up to the fact that it needed replacing. It was twenty years old. New ones give way more power, and are much quieter. Another problem was my prop shaft, which was leaking more than it should be. My starboard running light also needed replacing, I needed to do some varnishing and change the fuel filters on my engine. I needed to find work so I could pay for it all.

Out looking for boat parts to make repairs, I had a very frustrating day, walking miles through the industrial part of George Town in flip-flops in very hot and humid weather, going round in circles and seemingly accomplishing nothing. I made it to Barcadere marina, had a shower and cooled down. In the chandlery I managed to find a fuel filter for my Yanmar, and another filter in a place round the corner. Back on the boat though, when I drained the bowl I managed to drop the plug nut into the bilge, and just couldn't reach it, so I needed a new filter bowl, which was very difficult to find. Eventually, I found one online and ordered it from the states. While changing all my filters I noticed that my seawater pump was leaking. It's an important pump that keeps the engine cool, so I needed to fix it.

Feeling broke and grumpy, it seemed like I was going two steps forward and one step backward, as soon as one thing was fixed something else broke.

I went to Marine Diesel, the Yanmar place in Morgan's Harbour, and asked about parts for my engine. Billy, the owner, later drove around to the boat and took some photos and checked the numbers. I ordered a new raw water pump and a new mixing elbow kit. I needed to spend some serious time and about a thousand dollars on engine maintenance. Otherwise it looked in fine shape, he said.

Dominica got badly hit by hurricane Erica. Meanwhile, a squall, a little bit of Erica, passed over Governor's Creek in the night and all hell broke loose. There were very strong winds, heavy rain and lots of lightening. I started dragging to the dock, so I quickly got lines and fenders tied, then jumped ashore at the last minute with the lines and another fender and fought to get the boat tied secure. Another boat came loose and ended up in the mangroves, and the police boat was washed up on the dock. Next up was hurricane Grace, although that was predicted to fizzle out before it reached the Caribbean.

Hurricane Ivan in 2004 was the last major hurricane to hit Grand Cayman. Although Cayman Brac got hit really badly in 2008. The Cayman Islands don't really have a hurricane hole. Whereas Jamaica has the massive Blue Mountains, and so Port Antonio is protected, the Caymans are very low lying. Their only advantage is that they are so far west; hurricanes tend to have turned north before they get this far.

Sheldon, the harbour master I'd made friends with, told me there was an old mooring – two big concrete blocks, very near to where I was anchored, so I went snorkelling to try to find it and attach a line. I spent hours looking all over the lagoon floor but just couldn't find it.

I did, though finally manage to get a new outboard – my new pride and joy, a two and a half horsepower Suzuki four stroke. Although I can hear Tom saying, 'Don't ever get a four stroke,' and I loved having five horsepower, it was such a good deal. The engine is second hand, but practically new; it had only been used once and still needed breaking in. It was bought from the local Suzuki dealer and was still under warranty; basically it was a new engine with thirty percent off. The owner, Clifton, had bought it three months ago with the idea of putting on the back of a little plastic inflatable (not really a proper dinghy; it didn't have a transom and was more like a beach toy). The engine was, of course, too heavy and too powerful. I decided to get it after asking around at marinas and checking e-cay, the local classifieds webpage for cheaper ones. I was desperate; not having a proper tender was a real nightmare and also dangerous. Even with oars, a strong wind could blow you out to sea or stop you getting to shore. Also, arriving by paddle, actually a broom handle taped to a flipper, wasn't cool.

Clifton wanted way more than I could afford, but he accepted my very low offer, I feel more respectable and properly equipped with my new outboard, even though the guys at the dock made fun of my two and a half horsepower. I locked it to the dinghy with a bike lock and used some cable to lock the dinghy to docks. Grand Cayman felt much safer than Jamaica, but I'd decided to go overboard on outboard security. The outboard was actually suffering from not being stored properly. Clifton told me he hadn't emptied the fuel tank when he'd stopped using it. So I went to the Suzuki dealer and arranged for them to come to the boat and clean the carburettor and fuel jet. Even though the engine was still under warranty they charged me sixty bucks, but I thought it was better to fix it before it caused another problem, and it was good to get the Suzuki mechanic to show me so I could do it next time.

For a change of scenery, I motored out of Governor's Creek, out of North Sound and headed round the island to West Bay and Seven Mile Beach. I loved the calmness of the creek, but missed the clear water of the open ocean. I went snorkelling over another wreck, the *Kittiwake* – a submarine rescue ship in sixty feet of water, the funnel was only about fifteen feet from the surface. It was bigger, and in better condition than the *Keith Tibbetts*, and even more impressive. I saw lots of rays and parrotfish. Looking up from the bottom of the sea to see three Eagle Rays swim past above you is a magically sight. They look like birds flying over your head.

Most days I went for a walk along Seven Mile beach, which was just over the road from the Yacht Club. There were two nice bars quite near: Tiki Beach and Calico Jack's, and both had showers and Wi-Fi. Further south, the Marriott and Ritz Carlton were nice; I liked the Marriott Jacuzzi. One day I went to the Westin – my favourite hotel so far, and chilled in the pool, the showers and the air-conditioned lobby. I had a long list of boat maintenance jobs, as well as day-to-day things to do, like grocery shopping, laundry and filling up with water, etc. I try to cross at least one thing each day, except on Sundays. Then I take a break to laze around and enjoy the Caribbean.

On a search for a launderette (also usually a good source of free books) one day, I went to Camana Bay, a beautiful, and expensive new shopping centre and office development. I found free Wi-Fi and power in one of the cafes and a farmers' market. The launderette, *Fluff and Fold* was more like a dry cleaners, but I did find the Book Tree – which had a great book swap, and I got some new books, including *A Trip to the Beach*, a book by an English couple who started a restaurant in Anguilla. In the evenings out in the Creek I often listened to the radio and read a book. I could get Wi-Fi from Morgan's Restaurant, which was run by Jane, an English lady and her Dutch husband. I'd been there for drinks and a meal and made friends when I introduced myself as owner of the blue sailboat anchored in front of their garden.

One of my favourite places on Grand Cayman was West Bay – a really nice place to wander around. There was a nice beach with private showers and a dinghy dock, and also a good supermarket. It seemed like it hadn't changed much over the years and there was still an old Caribbean feel. I bumped into my pirate friend. Well, he'd called out to me from across the street, and we hung out for a while. I often went to the West Bay launderette so I could have a swim while I waited for the washing. I also went to a roadside café and got mashed potato, mac and cheese and coleslaw for three bucks.

My propane ran out, so I needed to get it filled. It turned out that I would need to take my bottle to the gas company in George Town. I managed to fill it, although it was very confusing asking for the gas station. I didn't mean gasoline but propane. To add to the confusion, it turned out gas (petrol) stations do actually fill gas bottles with propane, but not the kind of bottle I had. I needed the Home Gas depot. Once I found it, they filled it right there in front of me. I then discovered carrying a full bottle of gas was not allowed on buses so no bus drivers would let me on. I found a plastic duty free shopping bag and eventually carried the bottle disguised as a Heineken beer keg onto a bus stop and back to the marina.

Seemingly out of nowhere hurricane Joaquin popped up. When I checked passage weather, there was a huge red blob just on the other side of Cuba, over the Bahamas. This afternoon it brought fairly strong winds, but coming from the West – the opposite of the usual trade winds. My anchor chain flipped round one hundred and eighty degrees, which was not good. Sure enough I slowly started to drag. This time I was drifting towards rocks and an expensive motor yacht. And this time my engine wasn't working because I was still waiting for a fuel filter part.

I quickly got my spare anchor and jumped in the dinghy. I dropped it about fifty feet away, led the rode back to *Sonic Boom*, jumped aboard and pulled it tight. Luckily it held really well and I sat in the middle of the channel to the marina in everybody's way. A couple of boats went past,

'Hey, you can't anchor there.'

'Why are you moored there? You should move.'

Unable to move, I smiled and waved. Eventually, I managed to get a tow to the dock and tied up, just minutes before the winds kicked up to twenty knots and heavy rain poured down with lots of thunder and lightning. It was another very lucky escape.

After Joaquin, *Sonic Boom* was tied up on the dock shared by the Yacht Club and Morgan's Restaurant and attracted a steady stream of visitors. I made friends with the Honduran fishermen on *Pescadora*, some locals on a party catamaran and Rodriguez – the Indian security guard who was from Goa. I also made friends, kind of, with an iguana, which sneaked on board. He could stay if he caught mosquitos. I went to Morgan's and had a Skype interview with one of the managers of Diver's Supply who was actually in Canada and was offered a job in their store – sales and equipment servicing. It was great news and a massive relief. It would be good to get some income, pay down credit cards and save a bit for what would come next. I had to apply for a work permit but, luckily, Diver's Supply do it with their own lawyers. I was slightly concerned about the boat being my address and possibly having to pay import duty on it if I stayed in Grand Cayman beyond a certain length of time.

There was a fair amount of paperwork for my work permit, including a request for UK police clearance. I managed to find that online, apply, pay and have it sent to me here by my sister. I'd paid express police and mail fees to have it delivered to my sister within a couple of days. Unfortunately she'd then it to me standard mail. Two weeks later, I first got a message in the post from Parcel Force stating that my police clearance had arrived on the island and should be delivered soon. The next message from Parcel Force stated that the police form couldn't be delivered because the envelope was too big to fit in the post box, so it would be returned to the UK. I quickly went to George Town post office, which then sent me to Seven Mile post office. It turned out Seven Mile post office was in West Shore Plaza – the same as Diver's Supply. Actually they shared the same building – the post office was literally two doors down. I managed to get it before it was returned. I submitted all my other paperwork and I bought a prepaid phone, so I had a contact number. Now I had to leave the island, while the permit was processed.

I booked a flight to Jamaica for the next morning. My flight was to Kingston. From there I planned to head to Negril where I knew there were cheap hotels. I wasn't sure how long it would take for the permit or how I was going to pay for everything. It was taking way longer and costing way more than I'd expected. Hopefully I'd make it back to Grand Cayman, start work and get my first pay check soon. The flight time was just over forty-five minutes, which beat a three-day sail by just less than three days.

I arrived in Kingston at eight. I was hoping to meet someone going to Negril, but had no such luck. So I got a bus from the airport to downtown Kingston, then another to New Kingston. There I had to wait five hours for the bus to Negril. After all the scare stories I'd heard, Kingston didn't seem so bad. I was expecting total chaos and some danger, but I managed everything fairly smoothly and didn't get shot. The Knutsford Express took five hours to get to Negril. I checked into Traveller's Beach Resort for my first night, which I'd booked on Expedia for forty bucks. The next day, I looked for something cheaper. All I could do now was wait until I heard my permit was ready. I prayed it wouldn't take too long and I didn't run out of money before I got back to Grand Cayman.

It was great to be back in Jamaica, even though I was struggling financially and still anxiously waiting to hear news from Grand Cayman. I checked into Judy's Guest House, a lovely backpackers' hostel in West End up the hill, overlooking the sea. There was a beautiful garden and outdoor bathtubs, and it was only twenty bucks a night. After three nights, my work visa came through – what a relief! I searched for flights and ended up on a Sunday night flight from Kingston. It saved me having to pay for another hotel room, although for my last night I didn't even have a room; I was in a garden hammock for ten bucks.

I took the early morning bus, which broke down, and ended up taking six hours to New Kingston. Then I managed to share a taxi to the airport with two Germans. I wasn't so sad to be leaving Jamaica this time, since I'd be living on the next island and I'd definitely be back again soon. I arrived back in Grand Cayman without a penny so I walked home from the airport. I was completely broke and still had food, bus fares and laundry to pay for. There would be lots of walking, hand washing clothes and not much food for the next week or two, but I'd made it somehow. On my birthday, I went to Seven Mile beach to celebrate. Work started the next day at Diver's Supply.

I borrowed a mountain bike from Rodriguez, my Indian friend, so getting to work wasn't a problem. My first week of work at Diver's Supply went really well and I started making commission. One day when I was cycling to work, there were people lining the streets cheering me on. I was smiling and waving back when lots of racing bikes flew past and I remembered there was a triathlon on that day. It was nice to be cheered on to work though, I thought until I turned off their route and everyone started shouting, 'You're going the wrong way,' instead. On my first day off, I went to the beach, took a shower and went to the super market. At last it was payday – another cause for celebration. Hitting rock bottom at least meant the only way was up.

I went to customs again, they were happy and I had another extension for *Sonic Boom*, which cost one hundred dollars, to go with my work visa from immigration. I had a bank account at Cayman National Bank and a local phone number, so it felt like I'd really moved to Grand Cayman. *Vida Libre* and my friend Dana arrived from Jamaica and we went to watch the fireworks and the start of Pirates Week. Pirates Week was a big deal in Grand Cayman; it was like a carnival and a perfect way to celebrate my new home. There were lots of people dressed as pirates and lots of rum drinking. The next day, there was a pirate invasion and the Governor was kidnapped. Later, there was a big pirate parade and lots more rum drinking. I managed to meet lots of pirates.

Another nasty storm passed right over Governor's Creek – thirty-five to forty knot winds, lots of lightening and torrential rain. *Sonic Boom* started dragging again, but with two anchors down it was really difficult to do anything. I motored into the wind first, then ditched one anchor and hauled up the other, but I got anchor rode wrapped around my propeller, so my engine cut out. I jumped in the dinghy and managed to cut it free. Luckily (for me), I had been headed towards (and bumped very gently) Dana's boat, so she jumped in her dinghy and helped me to the dock. The next day, I retrieved my spare anchor and freed my propeller. There was no damage done; I'd had another lucky escape.

In November, I celebrated my second anniversary – two years aboard *Sonic Boom*. I'd been to thirty-three islands. I went diving with Ben from Diver's Supply. We got free rental equipment and cheap tanks from work and dove at Macabuca, one of the most popular shore dives on Grand Cayman. It was amazing, so many fish; we saw grouper, parrot fish, eels, turtles and huge tarpon that swam round in circles in an underwater cave. We went down to about sixty feet for just less than an hour. Swimming in crystal clear and very warm water, amongst beautiful coral and caves, was lots of fun and cost just eight bucks for the tank.

There were lots of reasons to celebrate: hurricane season was over, at last; it was Thanksgiving and Christmas was on the way. At work, we closed early and had an early office Christmas Party at Casanova's Italian restaurant. We had a great view of fireworks that were actually for the end of Pirates week, lots of good food and wine and presents. As well as a Secret Santa, all staff got one hundred dollars from Greg, the owner, to spend in the store. I bought an Oceanic diving mask and a pair of Mares fins.

In the creek, the glow worms were back. I was told it was the second night after a full moon when they appeared. Glow worms are tiny little worms that you can't see, but that leave little spirals of bright phosphorescence and clouds of bright green light behind them as they swim along just beneath the surface. I loved the calm water and safety of the creek, but I was missing the clean water and convenience of Hog Sty Bay and Whitehall Bay, so I motored round to George Town and picked up a buoy next to Dana. It was nice to be in clear water, above coral and thousands of fish, snorkelling off the back of the boat. The two of us went to Cheeseburger Reef, just a hundred yards away. It was so nice being moored off George Town, which was convenient for laundry and supermarkets. Each day, I dinghied to the dock outside the Lobster Pot, a nice waterfront restaurant and one of the best dive centres and then cycled to work. Work was much closer than when I was at the Yacht Club.

I tied up to one of five free public mooring balls in Whitehall Bay, so it was the same price as Governor's Creek, but the water was crystal clear and I was near lots of good snorkel spots. The only problem was that it could be rolly. Even without wind or waves, there were often big swells, low and spaced apart, that I imagined were from some distant storm and that made my boat rock like crazy. Still, I loved Whitehall Bay. It was nice not to be on my anchor, near town, and especially cool being able to snorkel off the back of the boat. My new fins and mask were awesome. It was also interesting to watch the cruise ships coming in and going out again. Sometimes five were anchored off George Town. The cruise ships dropped anchor under pilot guidance and passengers were ferried to shore for the day. They didn't stay overnight.

There was a lot of debate about cruise ships after a video of a cruise ship anchor destroying coral went viral and The Daily Mail picked up the story. There was a controversial plan to build a dock so the ships wouldn't have to anchor. There was a widely criticised environmental impact study. Then Paul Allen, one of the founders of Microsoft, ran into trouble anchoring off George Town when his mega-yacht *Tatoosh* dragged its anchor and Grand Cayman's coral reef hit the headlines again. He was fined half a million dollars even though he'd apparently been instructed where to drop anchor. He paid for restoration to the damage caused and funded new moorings for mega-yachts so they could avoid anchoring. I met some of the divers from *Polaris*, the company who carried out the reef restoration, in Divers Supply. Scuba diving was still an important part of The Cayman Islands, even though the reef had sadly been deteriorating for years. Pollution, especially from sun tan lotion, anchor damage and over fishing had taken their toll. Conch and turtle were terribly over fished. The turtle sanctuary on the island actually sold turtle meat, which was still widely eaten on Grand Cayman.

There had been lots of rain, and it looked like a big storm was coming, so on my day off I sailed back around the island and into Governor's Creek. I was going really fast until I approached the main channel into North Sound and hit strong winds and waves head on. It took an hour to motor the last couple of miles; then once I was through the channel, I put up my sails again and headed west to Governor's Creek and beautifully calm waters.

Just as one set of paperwork had been done, I seemed to get another. My three-month work visa ended in January, so I went and got my application form for the next one, which would be for a year. There were pages of forms to fill, plus a medical requiring an X-ray and a blood test for HIV. So I went to a doctor's and an X-ray clinic. Both were full of people needing medicals and X-rays for their work visa applications. My health insurance covered the medical and blood test, but I paid thirty-five dollars for the X-ray.

One of the questions on my immigration form was, 'Do you live in a house, apartment or hotel?' Unfortunately, it was a tick-the-box question; otherwise, I would have just put "no". Did I own or rent was another tricky one. They required a lease agreement signed by a landlord so I arranged to go into the marina and spoke to Sheldon and Karl at the Yacht Club to get the necessary signatures on the various forms. I signed a lease and moved into slip D7. I hadn't been in a marina since Aruba, six months ago. It was nice to be surrounded by friends, and amenities, but it was also a four hundred dollar monthly bill I couldn't really afford.

Making the most of being on a dock, I scrubbed the decks, washed down the cockpit and filled up with fuel and water. Ben from work dropped off two tanks and his gear ready for a dive we'd planned for Christmas Day (a rare day off). It was a luxury being so near land, connected to a water supply. I was able to finish the varnishing and fit my new engine parts; a new mixing elbow and a raw water pump. I also tightened the stuffing box on the propeller shaft. That with the new fuel filters and a bit of a clean-up, and I was very happy with my engine. Although being in the marina had been nice, one night I came home to find a rat on board. Not good. Ate my chocolate and crapped on my seat (the rat did).

After a month, immigration approved my one-year visa, so I left the dock and went back on my anchor in the creek to save money. I went to immigration and got my passport stamped with my work permit. There should be no more immigration hassles for a year. Meanwhile, Customs said after six months I needed to either leave or pay import duty on *Sonic Boom* – they wanted two thousand dollars, payable immediately. So I reluctantly paid Customs two thousand dollars import duty on *Sonic Boom*. Ouch.

On Christmas Day morning, I sailed round to West Bay with Ben and Tracy and met up with Dana. We picked up Daniel and Kayla and went for a dive on the Kittiwake. I went to shore to get Davide, who brought some amazing homemade pasta and we all had lunch. Then went for a second dive off Cemetery Beach. There were loads of tropical fish, beautiful purple fan coral, I saw a porcupine fish and a huge turtle swam right up to me. It was like swimming in an aquarium. It was lots of fun diving with a group of friends, making each other laugh underwater, I nearly choked.

After the second dive, we had a few beers and were relaxing on Dana's boat watching the sun go down when I noticed the sun going down and realised we only had an hour or so of light left. I told everyone they needed to gather their stuff up, I needed to get everyone to shore. Since we'd moved the boats, West Bay dock was a good twenty-minute dinghy ride away. Dana offered to help with her dinghy so we could get all the dive equipment to shore too. I took a group back to *Sonic Boom* and then headed to the dock. When we got there we unloaded the dinghies, said goodbye and headed back. Ben though, called me back. He'd forgotten his keys, so I took him back to *Sonic Boom*, he grabbed his keys and we set off again for the dock. The sun had now set, but it was still light. By the time I'd got to the dock, dropped Ben off and turned around though, it was dark.

I headed home but after twenty minutes still couldn't spot *Sonic Boom*. I carried on, then went back, and still couldn't find my boat. I stopped and thought about what to do. The wind and current were pushing me out to sea. I was very low on petrol and didn't have any spare. Nor did I have a torch, whistle or drinking water. I didn't have anything. The thought of spending a night drifting out to sea was frightening. I would be impossible to see in the dark, Dana wouldn't miss me until tomorrow, if then, so it would probably be two nights before even a search party was sent. I had to find *Sonic Boom*.

I couldn't believe how stupid I'd been to end up in such a ridiculous situation, but one that could turn dangerous very quickly. I stayed calm and decided to keep looking, but to head into shore. I wanted to try and remain within swimming distance in case my fuel ran out. I mentally positioned *Sonic Boom* and was sure I was too far down Seven Mile beach. Slowly, I motored the dinghy northwards parallel to the beach and about quarter of a mile off it in almost pitch-blackness. There were a few sailboats moored. Their lights had been camouflaged by the lights onshore behind them, but now that I was a bit closer to shore and looking away from the shore lights, I could make out the boat lights. I passed one or two boats I didn't recognise but felt better because I could swim to them if my engine stopped. After ten minutes I spotted *Vida Libre* a few hundred yards ahead. From there I knew *Sonic Boom* was a couple of hundred yards further out to sea.

Dana later left to Cuba and I sailed back around the island. I was sad to see her go and was very tempted to go with her. On my day off I motored across North Sound to Kaibo beach. I wanted to give my engine a good run. It was working better than ever, the new exhaust was giving me more power. I tied up on Kaibo Pools dock and went for a snorkel. I saw lots of starfish and a couple of stingrays. I swam under *Sonic Boom*, checked my zinc and cleaned my prop. My zinc needed replacing, but my bottom paint still looked good, with no growth or barnacles. I had lunch at Kaibo restaurant, went for a walk around, had another swim and headed back to Governor's Creek.

After a couple of weeks, I sailed back round to George Town. When I arrived there were no free mooring balls, so I tied up to a dive boat buoy. Port authority came around the next morning and asked me to move on to a different buoy; one right in the main harbour, close to shore, in front of all the waterfront bars and restaurants. Along with all the cruise ship passengers, the port authority boat was also watching nearby. I went very slowly and, fifty yards out, shut off my propeller completely and turned into my final approach. I got my hook and went to the bow. *Too slow, not enough power*, I thought I wasn't going to reach, but *Sonic Boom*'s bow came to a stop just touching the buoy. Perfect. I grabbed the loop, fed my mooring line through and threw it back into the water, just as the wind pushed me back out and pulled the lines tight. The port authority boat came right over and drew up alongside. The crew were all smiling and shaking their heads. The captain told me that was one of the best he'd seen,

'Boats with four crew, all with radios, not been able to do that.'

I was very happy.

Some of the other mooring balls eventually freed up and I moved to a quieter spot in Hog Sty Bay alongside *Atlantis*, the submarine and in front of my friends *Jolly Roger*. *Jolly Roger* was actually a two-thirds replica of Christopher Columbus' fifteenth century galleon *Nina*. I was above a beautiful reef and there were big blue parrotfish and tarpon swimming right under my hull. It was so nice to be back in clear water and snorkelling off the boat every day. I cleaned my propeller and replaced my zinc.

Another advantage of being on the west coast was the spectacular sunsets. One cloudless night, the setting sun touched the horizon and I saw my first evergreen flash. Just as the last spot of sun disappeared behind the horizon, there was a bright green flash, not quite as spectacular as the very big green flash in *Pirates of the Caribbean*, but amazing none the less. I'd doubted whether they actually happened but always looked out for them at sunset anyway. At work the next day, Davide told me his friend had also seen it.

I usually left my dinghy on the dock next to the Catboat Club. Catboats are traditional Cayman Islands sailboats, usually with one mast at the bow, often used for turtle fishing. My friend Tyrone told me the story of how they got their name. Long ago a local man built a small boat and one day found his cat asleep inside. She'd given birth to kittens and so was very protective of the boat, which became known as the catboat.

It was fun listening to the VHF radio in the morning and the conversations between port authority and the arriving cruise ship captains. A small pilot boat went out to guide the cruise ships to a specific spot with a sandy bottom away from the reef where there was twenty-two feet of water under their keel.

'Captain, keep comin', you got another ten meters to go.'

'Well, I really must insist on eight meters under my keel.'

'No problem, will be cool man, just a little more.'

'Now that's enough, I'm showing seven meters under the keel. I will stop here.'

'All right, go ahead and drop your anchor, 'tis a good spot.'

Once the anchor is down, a scuba diver goes down to make sure it is in sand and holding. Cruise ships have enormous anchors – the size of SUVs, on chain as thick as a tree.

'Captain, we be sendin' a diver down now to check your anchor.'

'Roger that.'

'Well, captain, the diver can't seem to find your anchor, him go check again.'

'I seem to be holding. Over.'

'He can't see it but if you're happy it should be all right. Have a good day. Over.'

I went snorkelling with Tyronnie and Mario over the Wreck of the *Cali* – a two hundred and twenty foot four-mast schooner that sank in 1944. We saw lots of fish and some huge tarpon. I was swimming along watching a parrotfish below, when I looked up and saw a huge Eagle Ray right in front of me. I spent another day off snorkelling off the wreck of the *Gamma*. On the fourth of July, Tye and Mario got married at the church in George Town. It was absolutely beautiful; the church looked lovely, the vicar was very cool and all the guests were given little silver wedding bells.

On my way back to Governor's Creek, about an hour after leaving George Town anchorage, I heard an engine alarm and saw the low oil warning light had come on. I switched off the engine and discovered all my oil had sprayed out through the dipstick port. I refilled the oil and everything went back to normal. A bit scary, very messy and I wasn't entirely sure why it happened. I continued back and anchored in Governor's Creek next to a catamaran called *Seismic Wave*, which seemed like a good match for *Sonic Boom*.

I spent a day off doing maintenance. My head had been leaking, so I took the pump apart, cleaned it and tightened everything up. No more leaks, but it was looking worn. I'd serviced over a year ago in Trinidad, so I ordered a new one. Greg, who also owns a boat, helped me get shipped. I also ordered a new starboard running light and a replacement furlex screw. I installed a new engine ignition switch after mine broke. I fitted a new vented loop on my exhaust hose, and so my cooling system was now completely refurbished. I also made a new mosquito net for my fore hatch. Then I took the boat out into North Sound, cleaned the hull and propeller and tightened my zinc.

I did more varnishing and finally my teak was starting to look better. Everything had five coats of varnish. I'd ideally wanted to get nine coats on everything. It still wasn't as good as I had it in St Martin. I'd left it way too late. What should have been just a light sand and a few quick coats, was instead a major headache. I had to take everything back to bare wood and start all over again. There wasn't much teak left, after over forty years of wear it was very thin. Replacing it would be expensive.

I went battery shopping with Davide. My starter battery had died. It was almost exactly five years old. I replaced it with the same Napa battery, for one hundred and twenty dollars. Harbour House Marina has the best chandlery on the island, and in July they had a boat show and a thirty per cent off sale. I went with Super Mario and Tamarion and a long list of all kinds of exciting things to buy, but ended up spending nearly everything I had on four deep cycle batteries.

Exploring the canals and lagoons I discovered Lime Tree Bay and a new place to moor *Sonic Boom* for a while. I motored along a canal to Lime Tree Bay and tied up to Living the Dream's hurricane mooring in Mitchell's Creek. Living the Dream were one of the best dive centres on the island. Luckily my new mooring was much closer to work, because someone had stolen my bike. It was the first time I'd been next to a golf course and strange to be on the boat and hear people tee off. I also noticed birds singing. One night a loud flapping sail sound woke me up, which was, I eventually worked out, a flag on the green next to me. I think it was partly because I was usually anchored next to a beach listening to waves. Living on a sailboat you're always listening out for strange sounds.

Some more big storms passed over and around Grand Cayman, bringing strong winds and thunder and lightning. Hurricane season had officially started. The local newspaper came with a special guide to hurricane season 2016. Tropical Storm Earl passed close by Grand Cayman. Conditions were bad enough for Living the Dream to want their hurricane buoy back. So I tied up at the Yacht Club for a stormy night, next to my friends on *Jolly Roger*. It was always good to see them. I moved quite early, before things got too bad and then watched as boats started dragging and the dock filled up. I helped Leonardo, an Italian sailor, tie up his huge yacht after he abandoned his anchor. A real bare bones pirate, the boat's name had worn off, and so had all the paint. There was no glass in most of the port holes and holes in the dash where the instruments should be.

He came crashing into the dock, I heard something break off and fall into the water as I secured his lines. He didn't have any fenders. After a couple of seconds in shock, I quickly went to get one of my fenders while Leonardo tried to hold off his probably ten-ton boat from being smashed against the concrete dock by big waves and thirty knot winds. I tied a fender to the dock and watched the huge boat squash it flat like a pancake. Leonardo went off to try and borrow some more.

Jamaica was my nearest hurricane hole, way too far away. There were plenty of mangroves nearby, but I wanted a better hurricane plan than hiding behind a bush if I was going to spend another hurricane season in the zone. I spoke to other boat owners to find out what their hurricane plans were. The preferred options were: haul out (if a storm was announced there'd be a big rush to the cranes and haul out fees would go crazy), tie up to a hurricane mooring in the creek if you owned one (I didn't), tie up in the mangroves. During hurricane Ivan in 2004, Grand Cayman completely disappeared from radar for a while, as the storm surge submerged the whole island. At the marina, Dock A ended up seven miles away in the mangroves with all the boats still attached. Flying debris was a major concern. Two hundred mile an hour coconuts can cause a lot of damage.

Although I'd prefer the mangroves to being on a dock, as a possible alternative hurricane hole, I looked at Crystal Harbour, a luxury development just round the corner from me. All the houses had wooden docks at the end of their gardens. I would be out of any waves, facing east and sheltered (by tall buildings) from the north and west. I could centre myself in the canal, run lines either side and set a spider's web. A major problem with being on a dock, is the sudden and massive rise in water level. The ropes will snap when the boat goes up too far, or cleats will break. Before Hurricane Ivan the yacht club thought they'd solved this with posts and floating docks, so the lines could move up with the water. However for Ivan the posts weren't tall enough. During the storm surge the boats were floating above the submerged posts but still tied to them so the hulls bounced on the posts until they burst through, eventually leaving some boats skewered. New posts now rise twelve feet above the water.

I checked the weather forecasts every day. There had been a big disturbance brewing in the Atlantic the previous week, which passed St Lucia and turned into tropical storm Mathew. It then very quickly became a category five (the maximum) hurricane and was heading to the Caymans. The forecast was for it to soon turn north to Jamaica and pass along the east coast. But even with that path Cayman Brac and Little Cayman are forecast to get waves of nine to twelve feet. I talked to other boat owners; we were all very nervous. The people at Red Sail moved all their boats to their safe haven and were on standby to take down their sails and masts. Hurricane Mathew finally turned north and I escaped one of the biggest hurricanes ever in the Caribbean. Poor Haiti suffered most damage, the eye of the storm passed over their west coast.

I went diving with Daniel on the Cobalt Coast – the north shore where Reef Divers were. Reef Divers were awesome, Julia and Will and Oli were lovely. The dive centre was immaculate, and the dive was amazing. We both had all our gear, so we just paid ten dollars each for two tanks. I had been to their dive centres on Little Cayman and Cayman Brac and all were also absolutely beautiful. We were going to go again the next day, but the waves had picked up so instead we went to Lighthouse Point and Dive Tech. Their building still had parts of the old architecture – thick antique wooden doors and canons. It was very pirate, I loved it. The onsite café was vegetarian (except for the lionfish it served). The dive was incredible. My favourite dive so far. There was a huge bronze sculpture by Simon Morris under the water. '*The Guardian of the Reef*' was half Roman soldier, half seahorse. At about eighty feet we saw a massive turtle, the size of a VW. We also saw a huge moray eel, a huge grouper took us to a lion fish that was hiding under a rock, and I think was very disappointed we didn't kill it, and another turtle that swam right over my head.

The PVC on my dinghy was worn so thin, in patches I could see the inner cloth. Leaks were popping up everywhere, so I kept my pump on board, but I needed to find a more permanent solution. I hadn't seen any second-hand inflatables, a new Zodiac like the one I had would be two thousand dollars, but I did find an eight-foot Walker Bay. I took it for a test run and liked it. My Suzuki engine wasn't too heavy for it. I was a bit wobbly at first, but I thought it would work. I liked that you could add a keel and a mast and sail. I managed to get the price down to five hundred dollars, including a huge pair of oars.

Pirates, this time online ones, managed to empty my Cayman National Bank account and steal my wages just three days after payday, apparently to play online poker. Cayman National Bank was very unsympathetic, but, luckily, because the transactions were in the US and I caught them so quickly (before any had been settled), Visa stepped in. Eventually, I got all my money back and a new card. It turned out that someone at Cayman National Bank had been selling customer data.

I went for my first dive using nitrox. I took the online PADI course with Daniel and then went for a two-tank boat dive on the North wall with Indigo divers. Our tanks were filled with a thirty-two per cent oxygen mix. Chris and Kate were great, it was a fun trip. Our first dive was Tarpon Alley and then we dove Blue Peter (named after the TV show that did some filming there). We saw lobsters and turtles and lots of sleepy stingrays, taking a rest from Stingray City.

At Stingray City, there was a sand bar where lots and lots of huge stingrays swam right up to people standing in about three feet of water, some feeding them squid. It is an amazing natural phenomenon that started years ago when fisherman used to clean their fish there and attract stingrays. Some people pick the stingrays up and hold them out of the water. Others kiss them for good luck. Stingrays don't have teeth but they can suck really hard.

I went for a two-tank boat dive with Tortuga Divers. Tortuga had their centre at Morritt's Resort, on the east end of Grand Cayman, a beautiful forty-minute drive from George Town. James had very kindly invited me. Our first dive was to High Rock, on the south coast. It was spectacular. Then we dove Big House, which was incredible. Swimming through tunnels in the coral, like secret passageways. It was the most colourful dive yet – lots of blue and purple sponges, some huge lobsters and tiny shrimp crabs. Nigel spotted and speared two lionfish, and not long after, an eight-foot nurse shark came to check it out. My calf was bleeding (blood looks like ink at sixty feet) from scraping some coral. One of the other divers was also cut. The shark was swimming amongst us until one diver tried to touch its tail; it swam off and the diver got told off. A few minutes later, it came back and a bigger reef shark also appeared.

I learnt a lot about sharks while diving in the Cayman Islands. I thought they were beautiful creatures, very inquisitive but also quite shy. The film *Jaws* has given them a reputation they don't deserve. Locals were terrified of them, even though there were no dangerous ones living in their waters. Customers came into the dive shop wanting to buy knives to protect themselves from sharks even though they were an endangered species. Siggy invited me to go diving with Ambassador Divers, who were currently celebrating twenty-five years. There was me and four other divers on their huge boat for a two-tank dive. We picked up buoys just off Seven Mile beach. The first dive was Holiday Inn drop off, then we went to Royal Palms ledge. Both were amazing dives; we saw stingrays, lionfish, an enormous crab, lots of colourful coral and sponges. Chris led the dives and was very cool. I tried out a pair of split fins and they were better than I thought they would be.

Every few months on Grand Cayman there was a Lion Fish Cull, a competition organised by all the dive companies. Over a weekend teams would go out and catch as many lion fish as they can. The aim was to reduce the numbers of lion fish which is an invasive species to the Caribbean. They feed on the babies of all the other fish and are a big threat. There were prizes for the most caught by number, and by weight, as well as prizes for the largest and for the smallest caught. One Sunday, I went with Daniel to Duke's Bar, where they were announcing the winners and holding the prize ceremony for the latest cull. At the bar, they were giving away various lion fish dishes, encouraging people to try it. Then they started the prize giving and up steps the winner of biggest lion fish caught. He stood and held the impressive fish in a classic pose and had his photo taken. Next was the winner for smallest fish and up steps the winner. Same pose but his fish is only fifteen millimetres, less than an inch long. It was tiny; we could barely see it as he held it up, pinching its tail between his thumb and finger. He didn't use a spear gun; he caught it with a spoon and a plastic bag. But he won the same prize money and got the loudest applause.

There was a nice cool breeze at night and no mosquitos. Some very big storms in the North Atlantic (Scotland would get battered), and one off Central America meant thirty-knot winds and big waves for a few days. Rough seas meant no diving, so I tried to catch up on some boat maintenance. I finally fixed my compass light and was very happy about that. In the end, I bought a tiny twelve-volt LED stick-on light for five bucks from Parkers, the best auto parts shop on the island. I changed my engine coolant and replaced my anchor locker drainpipe. I noticed my V belt was loose, but the bolt I needed to undo was stripped so I needed to get a turbo wrench.

The tiny gecko living on board *Sonic Boom* was happy at last. He climbed on board while I was in the marina ten months ago. I noticed him then, tried to explain he'd be happier on land and I flicked him off the deck into the water. He swam around for a minute but then climbed back on. So I left him alone and he seems to have forgiven me. I surprised him one afternoon while he was sunbathing on deck – he pretended to be invisible, then very slowly moved away. He looked happy enough, but I still wasn't sure he was going to like an overnight passage beating to windward.

The new fridge I ordered arrived. It had cost three hundred dollars. My new Dometic thermo-electric cooler was quite small – eighteen litres – and looked like a small cool box. It had a fan and compressor built in and used hardly any power (about two amps when it clicked on). At night it hardly came on at all. I always thought a solar powered fridge makes perfect sense; the brighter the sun, the more cooling you need, but the more solar power you get. I was trying not to get too excited, but I knew when I got the first cold beer I would scream and shout. I'd stopped buying dairy, but now I could keep eggs and cheese. I could also cook double portions and save the leftovers and save more money. I'd been happy to give up life without a fridge but I now had cold drinks and chocolate.

I fitted a new VHF radio and was also very happy with that. It was submersible and had an AquaQuake function. It also had built-in GPS – my coordinates were displayed on the screen, which meant that if I had a problem with my chart plotter I had back up for navigation. Online I got a ship radio license and registered the MMSI number, which meant if I lifted a small plastic cover and pressed a red button for three seconds, the radio would broadcast a digital distress signal with my location on a dedicated channel. So it was also back up for my EPIRB, which was registered with the US coastguard. Since *Sonic Boom*'s homeport is Troon, I had to register my MMSI number with UK coastguard. I hoped that meant I would get double rescued.

For my second Christmas on Grand Cayman I went for a dive at Sunset House with a group of friends – Richard, Norma, Joe and Mark, and we all wore Santa hats and took a group picture with the mermaid. *Amphitrite*, another Simon Morris sculpture, is a twelve-foot high bronze mermaid fifty-five feet down. I also got a bottle of Diplomatico Reserve Exclusiva Venezuelan Rum, my very favourite rum. Grand Cayman was covered in fireworks as all the hotels along Seven Mile Beach put on shows. So did Camana Bay and Kaibo. Sitting in my cockpit I was surrounded on all sides by fireworks. It was lots of fun, someone drank all my rum, apparently me.

I bought a couple of books about sailing that I'd found at the animal shelter shop and was already feeling much better about the lack of boat maintenance being done. The first book was John Kretschmer's story of sailing round Cape Horn in a Contessa 32 – my dreamboat. Contessas are very similar to Elizabethan 31s; both are tough heavy English sailboats built in Lymington in the 1970s, designed to be sailed in gale force conditions. Compared to *Gigi*, *Sonic Boom* is actually longer in the water, slightly narrower and heavier, has a longer keel, larger cockpit and more headroom. I am always interested to read about storm tactics. I smiled when Kretschmer wrote that when the wind went up from forty knots to fifty and waves up to fifteen feet, he added another reef in the main, rolled in the jib a bit more and maintained course. But what about in even worse conditions than that? Many sailors like him, and with boats as good as a Contessa, argue that in a hurricane out at sea, instead of going bare poles, the secret is to heave to. Both tactics were tried in my next book – the story of the 1979 Fastnet race and the deadliest storm in sailing history.

A strong northwester arrived in Grand Cayman and brought thirty-knot winds. They were not unusual for that time of year. The wind shifted to the west, and there were big breaking waves on Seven Mile Beach. I went for a swim and wiped out, twice. The waves also dumped tons of seaweed. The wind then shifted south, and finally was coming from the northwest. *Sonic Boom* was spinning around in Lime Tree Bay, for a while I was facing the opposite direction, bouncing up and down in, to be honest, small waves, but feeling very close to the concrete wall along the golf course. Very worryingly I noticed Living the Dream's hurricane buoy broken free and washed up against Crystal Harbour. Although I felt safe when I was tied to it, I wasn't entirely convinced I was. Much worse would be sailing along the north coast of Jamaica with massive waves pushing me onto it. It was a risk avoided by waiting until March.

On a beautiful sunny, calm day, with six cruise ships docked in George Town, I went for a two-tank boat dive off Seven Mile Beach with Lobster Pot. We first went to Round Rock, and then to the *Oro Verde* wreck, which was incredible. The story was that an old US Navy boat was bought by a Panamanian company to deliver bananas (which were green when loaded – hence green gold) to Miami. It was also smuggling marijuana (another green gold). There was a mutiny on the boat, the crew threw the captain overboard and then abandoned ship in North Sound. Later, Bob Soto bought it for a dollar, and then in 1980 it was sunk offshore from the Ritz as an artificial reef. Hurricane Gilbert smashed it against Paradise Reef, breaking it up and creating the most amazing dive site.

I met *Honey Ryder*'s friend Nancy, and five of her friends who were all staying at Beachcomber on Seven Mile Beach for a week's holiday. It was a very luxurious multi-million dollar apartment complex right on the beach, with amazing views from the balcony, a gorgeous pool, and lots of hot showers and Jacuzzis.

I took Vincent to Stingray City sand bar. On the way I filled up with water at the yacht club, and after a snorkel with the stingrays, we cleaned the hull and propeller.

After a quick shower we sailed back with ice-cold beers and some reggae. It was a fun afternoon but I noticed my anchor chain was now really bad. The shackle desperately needed replacing and lots of the chain was also really, really rusty, actually starting to flake and crumble. Also my Garmin chart plotter was dying. It worked but the screen had a big blob in the middle where I couldn't really see anything. So I had two expensive things I needed to buy; five hundred dollars for a new chart plotter, same again for one hundred feet of new chain.

I borrowed a pair of bolt cutters and trimmed my anchor chain. The rust was worse than I thought. I cut sixty feet off one end, and another sixty feet off the other, but had thirty feet of good chain left. I attached that to the anchor with a new shackle, and at the other end I had one hundred feet of nylon rode, eye spliced over a thimble and another new shackle. It looked good and meant a new, much lighter way of anchoring for me, that I was looking forward to. I installed the new Garmin chart plotter that arrived. I was hoping it would be an easy swap, but none of the cables or fittings were the same as my old one. I had to do rewiring and then mount it in my cockpit.

I had a very fun afternoon with Ambassadors; a two-tank boat dive off Seven Mile Beach – Spanish Anchor, and the Oro Verde. We saw a small nurse shark below us as we dropped down, and on the second dive, a big stingray, a turtle, lobsters, loads of parrotfish and angelfish, and lots of tiny, tiny things like shrimp, Christmas tree worms, some amazing sea anemones – feather dusters I think – they look like flowers but then quickly disappear when you get near. Jon led the first dive, and was very impressive underwater; it seemed like only his fins moved. I learnt how to do little frog kicks just using just my ankles to make small circles with my fins, and stay level.

For a couple of nights, on my way home, the moon hadn't risen, so it was pitch black, and my dinghy outboard left a bright green trail of bioluminescence as I motored back to *Sonic Boom* anchored in the middle of Mitchell's Creek. I went round in circles, dipped my hand in and watched the amazing bright green sparkles. During the day it wasn't so magical. I had to clean my propeller so jumped into Lime Tree Bay. Big mistake. I wore a long sleeved shirt, which helped (it was covered in shrimp when I got out), but I scraped off a whole load of crap and got attacked and stung/bitten by something all over my neck. Maybe jelly fish, or sea lice. So very itchy.

I loved living in Grand Cayman but staying in one place meant I wasn't really cruising anymore. The only advantage of having a boat was the free rent. And I had to put up with all the disadvantages – cramped living space, having to fill up with water. Although my commute to work was a nice dinghy ride to shore followed by a walk along one of the most beautiful beaches in the world, I still felt like I'd fallen back into the consumer life style that I'd been trying to find an alternative to. I started making plans to head east. I was now a long way away from the Windward Islands. Heading back there would mean going east – into the wind and waves, for over twelve hundred miles. I re-registered my EPIRB with the US Coastguard.

I filled up water, gasoline and diesel, and sailed to George Town for one last time before I left Grand Cayman. It was a beautiful day, my new Garmin GPS was amazing; a massive upgrade from my last one. When I got to North West Point, the wind dropped and the waves got very messy, so I tried to motor through it. Just like last time, I got engine warning lights and alarms. I shut off the engine and just drifted while I fixed the problem: my fan belt had snapped. Also the winch I hadn't serviced, seized up, so I needed to service that. When I finally got to George Town all the buoys were taken.

The Sea Shepherds were in town, on their way to Panama and another anti shark-finning mission. The Sea Shepherd Conservation Society is a non-profit marine wildlife conservation organisation and does great work. They gave a lecture at Guy Harvey's in George Town. Guy Harvey, the artist and wildlife conservationist, lived on Grand Cayman, I often saw him around. The Sea Shepherd's ship *John Paul DeJoria,* a one hundred and ten feet ex-coast guard patrol boat, was docked in George Town. It had a bright blue camouflage hull with shark's teeth painted at the bow. I met some of the crew, who were all very cool, when they came into the dive shop. It was very tempting to follow them and go through the Panama Canal.

Instead I would head east to Little Cayman. It was over eighty miles away, just a bit too far to make in a day, so it would be an overnight sail. The next passage after that, Little Cayman to Jamaica, was going to be another. Hopefully, I'd reach Montego Bay, but I'd settle for Negril. Then I planned to take a week to slowly hop along the north coast of Jamaica, with maybe some night sailing. At night cooling air falling down the mountains can create katabatic winds that make sailing east easier. I wasn't really looking forward to having to go so far so east. Going against waves, wind and current would make things hard. Especially the sail from Port Antonio to Haiti looked tough. I was hoping the wind might swing round to the north for that passage; otherwise I would sail north to Santiago de Cuba first, and then back down to Haiti. I planned to leave after breakfast on Saturday, hopefully arriving in Little Cayman for breakfast on Sunday. On Friday, the wind was forecast to shift slightly to the south, exactly what I was hoping for. I was also hoping it would shift back to the east for the sail to Jamaica.

Chapter 8
Hispaniola

I had a great sail to Little Cayman. It took twenty-four hours and was fairly drama free, although a shackle on my mainsheet traveller snapped, which was scary. A chunk of metal, a nut and a bolt flew past my face at a thousand miles an hour and out to sea. The boom swung out untethered, and I struggled to haul it back in and tie it down, and quickly find a new shackle. When I arrived, South Hole Sound looked a bit rough, so I tied up in Bloody Bay instead. Right outside a big white house, which belonged to the owner of Pizza Hut.

The next day I went for a two-tank boat dive with Pirates Point Divers. Their boat came round to Bloody Bay and I jumped on board. Captain Mishell was awesome. First, we dove Jackson's Bight and then Mixing Bowl. Both were absolutely spectacular. My favourite part was seeing a cleaning station. A huge grouper with its mouth fully opened, was letting little fish go inside and clean its teeth. Also, we saw turtles, stingrays, and lobsters. After the dives, I went back to Pirates Point Resort for a delicious lunch buffet, and a swim in their pool.

The following morning I set sail to Jamaica. It was almost twice as far as the sail to Little Cayman, but I hoped I could speed up a bit, and try get there in about thirty hours. The wind was still to the southeast, exactly where I wanted to go, so I had to head east, but was happy enough to get some easy easting. As I approached Cuba I figured it was time to head south, so I tacked and managed to go just a little east of south. Although I was going fast, I wasn't really going in the right direction so it was taking ages.

After a whole day and night, I was still only half way, then the wind dropped completely. I thought I'd have to motor sail the rest of the way, but luckily in the middle of the second night the wind picked up massively from the southeast and I sped along directly east. I accidently fell asleep at about one thirty, but when I woke up at four I was still speeding along on course, my self-steering system was working beautifully, *Sonic Boom* was perfectly balanced. A couple of cruise liners and a tanker on the horizon kept me alert until daylight.

Forty-eight hours after setting off, I approached Negril. A few dolphins came to say hello and play around with *Sonic Boom*, but I was only going four knots, and even though I clapped and whistled, they soon got bored and swam off. Or else they didn't like all the clapping and whistling. I anchored in Bloody Bay and tidied up a bit. The whole boat was covered in crumbs, spilt drinks and lots of salt. Even my ear was full of salt. The marine police came, boarded, stomped around a bit, checked my papers and then left. And then a thunderstorm brought heavy rain and I got a free boat shower – perfect. The next day, I left all sparkly clean again and motor sailed round to Montego Bay. Six hours later, I was anchored in Montego Bay.

I cleared in with customs and immigration at the Yacht Club, had a swim and a shower and meal and a beer. I was exhausted, but happy to be back in Jamaica. I decided to stay until Monday and avoid customs weekend overtime fees. In Jamaica, it was necessary to clear in and out of every port. Actually, customs were a real pain – even though I arrived on Friday at two and had finished with immigration by two thirty, I didn't finish with them until after three. So they charged me a sixty-eight dollars overtime fee because I cleared in after three o'clock.

I left Montego Bay Yacht Club early in the morning and sailed round to Discovery Bay, the first stop on my way to Port Antonio. Early on my engine broke down. I hate working on the engine under sail, and I wasn't able to fix it, but at least I found the problem – air in the fuel line. It soon became a very difficult sail. There was strong wind and big waves and it wasn't long before more things started to break under the heavy pounding. I lost the wind vane from the top of my mast. It got dark before I reached Discovery Bay, so rather than enter a new harbour and try to anchor in the dark without an engine, I hove-to and grabbed a couple of hours' sleep. Then I decided to carry on through the night and eventually made it to St Ann's Bay the next morning.

St Ann's Bay was miserable; the channel marker buoys were all missing. I had to surf in between waves breaking on reefs either side of the channel which I couldn't really see, because the water was cloudy, churned up by the waves. I had to quickly drop anchor and lower sail before hitting the beach – it's a very small bay, very exposed, and very rolly. There wasn't anything on shore, apart from Jamaica's loudest sound system that went off all night. Just as the music finished, at dawn, I pulled up anchor and motored through the channel, with my hopefully repaired engine (I'd patched a seal, and bled the lines), before the wind and waves picked up. Out in the open ocean, the wind was even stronger, the waves even bigger. I decided to give up trying to reach Oracabessa and sail to Ocho Rios, the next harbour along the coast. The cruising guide, which recommended St Ann's, had not recommended Ochi – too touristy, but it was lovely. A very sheltered bay, with a beautiful beach and lots of shops and restaurants. I rested for a few days.

After a couple of days of relaxation in Ocho Rios over the Easter weekend, lounging on the boat and strolling round the pretty town, I was ready to set sail again. I headed to Oracabessa, where there was Ian Flemming's house *Golden Eye*. Further along the coast at Port Maria, there was Noel Coward's house *Firefly*. I made it to Oracabessa and dropped anchor. It was a beautiful little bay, nice and sheltered. The wind dropped the following day, then non-stop heavy thundershowers kept me there for almost a week. Eventually, with still very little wind, I motor sailed to Port Antonio in about eight hours.

It was so nice to be back at Errol Flynn marina and Port Antonio, which was my favourite town in Jamaica. There were lots of cruisers in the bay, most going southwest, some going east. A huge classic yacht was on one of the docks and added to the feeling of being transported back in time. Actually it was the eight million dollar yacht *Germania*, which was a replica of a 1908 classic and incredibly impressive. It had one hundred and fifty foot masts. First up was immigration and customs, followed by a hot shower, then a beer and some food. Next was laundry, some boat work, lots of cleaning and more provisioning. It would be a long, difficult sail to Haiti, ideally I'd make Ile a Vache, but more likely I'd stop first at Anse d'Hainault, and the weather was nasty – thunderstorms and rain, so I was in no hurry to leave.

I took a bus to the Blue Lagoon, a very deep pool of very blue water nearby. It was the location for the film *Blue Lagoon*.

I also spent some time wandering around Port Antonio shopping for supplies. Restocked, refuelled and refreshed I sailed out of Port Antonio and out to sea early one morning. Almost straight away I was headed for a rainstorm, I couldn't avoid it so I reefed in and sailed through it. For the rest of the passage though, I managed to avoid three more huge storms. I sailed through the night, all the next day and spotted Haiti in the evening.

It was getting dark, and there didn't seem to be many lights on shore, so I couldn't see anything but I could smell the island – burning wood, cooking maybe. The wind died once I was in the lee of the island and I motored the last ten miles. Suddenly, I saw a little cluster of plastic bottles glide past my hull – fishing lines and lobster pots. I saw another, and some more, they were everywhere. Then I heard a horrible clanking juddering from my engine. I shut it off, and saw a couple of small water bottles and some string disappear off my stern. I couldn't go forward, tried reverse, nothing. I was stuck until morning, I thought, but I tried the engine again and got going. For five minutes, then exactly the same horrible crunching sound as more fishing lines wrapped round my propeller. I was trying to spot them but spotting a very small clear plastic bottle on a moonless night was nearly impossible. I jumped into the water with a torch and dove under the hull to cut the lines. Eventually, I was free and made it to the shoreline. I anchored off Anse d'Hainault, which looked fairly poverty stricken. Children without clothes on bits of wood and dugout canoes came to ask me for money, food, anything. I saw no engines, just lots of little sailboats. It seemed like a step back in time, or else a vision of the future.

The next morning I headed off to Ile a Vache. It was an exhausting sail, beating against the wind and waves, and the worst – current. *Sonic Boom* suffered more damage: my main sail ripped again – the same spot as last time; and my mast winch broke. Luckily the sail rip was just below the reef line so I could just reef in and carry on. I would try to fix the winch before I left Ile a Vache, or else I'd have to hoist sail by hand. All day I struggled, I was looking forward to the night. One way I'd found to go east more easily was to motor sail at night, using the katabatic winds coming off the land. It took me twenty-four hours to do sixty-six miles, to get to Baie a Feret, a beautiful bay and an old pirate base. The pirate Henry Morgan used to stay there. Overlooking the bay was the Port Morgan Hotel.

Port Morgan Hotel was an absolute oasis. It was very laid back, had a lovely swimming pool overlooking the bay, horses (not cows) roamed around the beautiful gardens. I had breakfast – eggs, toast, pancakes, juice, coffee, and grabbed some free Wi-Fi. I met the lovely French lady who opened the hotel in the 1980s. It was fun to listen to all her stories, of how she and her husband had sailed across the Atlantic with no GPS, came to Haiti and built the hotel. She also told tales of hurricane Mathew, which sat on Ile a Vache for days. She supplied me with some bread, eggs and drinking water for my onward journey. I also made friends with a Canadian yacht in the bay, *Calbodine*. On board was a family with three young children. They were headed east as well. My next stop was the Dominican Republic, and Bahia de las Aguilas – a beautiful deserted stretch of coastline.

It was a massive, forty-eight hour marathon sail from Ile a Vache. *Calbodine* followed me at the start but I lost them during the first night. I had more fishing wire around my propeller, which this time damaged my prop shaft seal, and I was now leaking seawater into the boat. It needed tightening, and probably re packing. I spent a night in the bay and set off at dawn the next day. In the morning, I saw *Calbodine* was anchored behind me, they must have arrived in the night. I knew better than to wake them, I wanted to stay but I was anxious to get to Barahona where I could finally fill up with water. I only had a couple of litres of drinking water left.

As I left for Barahona, I saw small dolphins off the bow. Everything felt good, but that was a feeling that wouldn't last long. The wind dropped after I made it through the Beata channel so it took me all night to get to Barahona. And I wasn't happy when I got there; actually, it was a real low point. So far I'd broken a winch, blown out my mainsail, I'd got water leaking in and fuel leaking out. I'd run out of water so I was hungry and thirsty. Barahona was a commercial port – filthy and fly infested. The sea was full of garbage – floating plastic bottles were everywhere. I tried to dodge them all because some were fishing floats. I anchored in the wrong place, the navy told me to move around the corner to a small bay, where I saw a dead dog float by. At least my pet gecko was happy; I found him sitting on my hatch mosquito net feasting on all the flies. The day before in some very bad waves, it was so funny, he came crawling out of the cabin into the cockpit looking very seasick, creeping very slowly, looked at me as if to say 'what the hell?' and disappeared into a towel – a good place to shelter.

To clear in I had to ferry four officials (customs, immigration, navy and intelligence) one by one to my boat (and give them all a beer). They took photos of my passport and papers with their phones; all I had to do was sign. Because I didn't have to use an agent, clearing in only cost me ninety dollars (plus a ten-dollar tip and my last three beers), instead of the two hundred and fifty it would have cost me elsewhere.

After a good meal and a night's sleep, I felt much better. I went to town and hit the supermarket. Then I put fifteen gallons of fresh water in my tank (free), swapped my empty five gallon jug of drinking water for a full one (cost less than a dollar), and bought ten gallons of diesel (about fifteen dollars). Things were cheap.

In Barahona, there were fresh fruit smoothie shops everywhere, and the most amazing grilled cheese sandwiches. The people were lovely, and parts of town were quite pretty – the houses were painted bright colours, there were parks and beautiful ocean views. After two days I felt fully stocked again and ready to move on, so I set off to Salinas, thirty miles east. After a beautiful sail in calm seas I arrived at a nice anchorage with a hotel, marina, beach and clear water. I stayed there for a couple of days, before heading to Boca Chica.

It was a long sail from Salinas to Boca Chica. I sailed right by Santo Domingo, the capital, which looked vast. When I arrived there were thirty-knot winds and thunderstorms so I was stuck there for a few days. Fortunately my friends on *Calbodine*, are here too, also waiting for the wind to calm down a bit. Soon they would turn south and head to the ABCs for hurricane season. My next sail would also be a very long one because I had to sail all around Puerto Rico and the US Virgin Islands without stopping. Even though I can travel to the States, and I've been to Puerto Rico before, unlike all the other Caribbean islands, non-US citizens are not allowed to go there by boat without getting a visa first.

I went with *Calbodine* to Santo Domingo for a day trip to the absolutely beautiful old colonial part of the city. It was all very pirate, restored forts canons, statues of Columbus. We had pizza for lunch in a very Mediterranean feel square. Then we found two chocolate museums and everyone was very happy. I bought big half-pound bars of organic dark chocolate. We left Boca Chica together and sailed thirty miles further east to Isla Catalina. It was a windy, overcast day, the sea looked black, and I didn't arrive until after dark; it wasn't much fun, but the next day I woke up next to a pristine white sandy beach and crystal clear water. I spent a great day lazing on the beach with *Calbodine*. Our next stop was Casa de Campo, a big marina ten miles further east for the next night and to clear out with customs and immigration.

Casa de Campo was a beautiful luxury marina, hotel, golf course and villa complex. The marina was made up of pretty painted houses modelled on Portofino. It was like being back in Europe, in a small Italian town. I went for a swim in the hotel pool which was set in a lush garden and had a waterfall. I went to the beach for the day with *Calbodine* and had fun with all of them. For lunch we drove to Altos de Chevron, an amazing recreation of a medieval village built in the 1980s. The whole place was like a film set, there was a beautiful old church, an amphitheatre and a great café that served salads in wooden bowls.

I was so sad leaving Casa de Campo. Partly because of all the thieving officialdom; customs, immigration, port authority, the navy, all wanted a twenty-dollar "fee" (cash only) to sign all my papers. But mainly because all of *Calbodine* lined up on the dock and waved me off. Martin and Annie and their lovely children Betsy, Nelson and Walace – they were so much fun, I hope I see them all again.

Chapter 9
The Virgin Islands

Big waves, strong winds, especially that night took my mind off *Calbodine* but made the going slow. All day, all night and I'd barely got half way across the Mona Passage. I was doing six knots, pounding through waves, but not really going in the right direction. Another day and night and I made it to Puerto Rico, still not even half way to Tortola.

The dreaded island of Caja de Muertos, an island that cannot be found, except for those who already know where it is. Anyway, I went there. Coffin Island seemed like a perfect place to stop after two days and two nights hard sailing from Casa de Campo. I was exhausted and still faced with days more non-stop sailing, I decided to make a semi illegal stop. I pulled up to the beach and dropped anchor. Only after did I notice a US Coastguard boat tied to the dock a mile down the beach, and sure enough they motored slowly over. All the US islands, unlike any other Caribbean Islands, require visas; I couldn't just arrive and clear in like everywhere else. However all they did was wave and say hello (although I'm sure they took a note of the boat name).

After a big bowl of spaghetti and a good night's sleep, I carried on. Another overnight sail and I made Isla Vieques. I decided to sneak into Sun Bay and hide, get another night's sleep and a good meal. I didn't go ashore and had the excuse that I needed to make emergency repairs. If anyone did want to see important things that were broken, I'd got plenty to show them. Some strong winds and lumpy seas, particularly the Mona Passage between the Dominican Republic and Puerto Rico had meant more damage. A rip in my jib was the scariest. It was a two-foot long tear that luckily wasn't growing. I had some damage too. I'd smashed my forehead with a winch handle, went face first into my bookshelf and got hit on the top of my head by the anchor locker lid. However, I was very happy that I'd soon reach Tortola.

I had a glorious sail across the Virgin Passage from Vieques to the Virgin Islands in light seas and twenty knots of wind. Six knots all the way in pretty much the right direction this time. After ten hours, I made St Thomas, but wasn't going to make Tortola before dark. I checked on the chart and saw Honeymoon Bay on Water Island would be a good place for another illegal overnight stop. That would mean the next day would be an easy twenty-mile sail to Tortola and I would avoid customs' overtime fees.

Finally, I sailed into Soper's Hole, BVI on Sunday afternoon. In a very crowded anchorage I squeezed in between all the boats on mooring balls, which were thirty dollars per night, and dropped my anchor. Then picked it back up and tried again not to be quite so close to another boat. Tortola was more than a thousand miles east from Grand Cayman. It had taken eight weeks, a bit longer than I'd planned, but I was very happy.

Arriving in Tortola I felt like I'd completed a big circle, I was back where I'd started. However I didn't feel any sense of completion. I wasn't ready to get off the boat and go back to live on land. In the 1968 Golden Globe, when Bernard Moitessier approached Plymouth and the finish line he was in the lead. Before he arrived he passed a bag containing his photos and journals to another boat and the message that he wasn't stopping. Everybody thought he was mad, as he kept sailing past the finish line and out to sea. He explained he was rejecting not only the commercialism of the race, but also its rules and restrictions and the loss of freedom they represented. Moitessier carried on across the Atlantic and all the way to the Pacific, finally stopping and going ashore in Tahiti.

I could understand Moitessier. Tortola didn't feel like an ending. I wanted to carry on. I'd discovered a new, very different way of life and a community of sailors "Living the Dream". It wasn't all umbrellas in rum cocktails; there was also lots of boat work and struggles with a lack of money. Fresh water and electricity could no longer be taken for granted and there was the threat of hurricanes in the summer. But the immense freedom, the luxury of morning swims in clear water, white sandy beaches, fresh coconuts and a oneness with nature more than made up for it.

First stop, after customs and immigration, and laundry, and food and drink, was the sail maker. I'd received quotes from Doyle and North Sails for a new mainsail, and both were around fifteen hundred dollars. That was nearly all my savings. In the BVI I will make critical repairs, but most I planned to do in St Martin where things were cheaper. I met with Bob Philips the sail maker for Doyle Sails, he took measurements and was generally awesome. He certainly knew a lot more about sails than I did and genuinely wanted me to have the best sail rather than the most expensive. The main thing I liked about Doyle sails was they are specifically designed for Caribbean conditions – extreme UV and constant trade winds. They were made in Barbados which meant free delivery to anywhere in the Caribbean. I ordered a new mainsail, which I would collect in St Lucia in a few weeks' time and gave him my jib to be stitched up.

I went to Nanny Cay, another very pretty marina, one of my favourites, for a swim in the beautiful pool there and a shopping trip to the chandlery. I had breakfast, bought some boat parts, swam and took a shower and chilled out. I still felt battered and bruised from so much sailing. Afterwards, I went to Road Town and bought a few more things, got a haircut and bought lunch from the bakery. I managed to hitch rides there and back pretty quickly. Later, I changed my oil and oil filter, checked my batteries, cleaned up the cockpit – washed the cushion covers, replaced a smashed speaker, and took down my tatted flag and put up a nice new ensign. I was feeling and looking a bit more ship shape. That evening a dinghy from a neighbouring yacht with a Texan flag came over to tell me how much they liked my boat,

'Y'all gat such a priddy boat.' They'd been taking pictures of *Sonic Boom* all day.

One day I took a ferry to St Thomas, and spent a great day on the beach and by the pool with Daniel, my dive buddy from Grand Cayman, and his fiancée Kayla. It was nice to spend time in the US Virgin Islands legally. I had a visa stamped in my passport when I got off the ferry. Ironically, that meant that I could now sail to the US Virgin islands on *Sonic Boom*. Some sailors had taken the ferry for that very reason – to get the stamp they needed so they could sail there. On returning I begrudgingly got another two-week stamp from BVI immigration.

I loved being in Soper's Hole, it is such a beautiful place. The waterfront buildings are all painted bright colours, and surrounded by steep hills covered in lush vegetation. It was nice to have a break from sailing. I like going to new places, but it was also really nice going back to a familiar anchorage, somewhere I'd been before. I planned to leave and go to Peter Island just a few miles away, one of my favourite islands, and spend some time relaxing on the beach. I left Soper's Hole and went to Peter Island where there's a beautiful beach and a luxury resort. I spent a day in the pool, lounging in beach chairs and watched the Champions League final on their huge TV. The next day, I left and headed to Leverick Bay in Virgin Gorda.

I was very reluctant to leave the British Virgin Islands and had nearly been persuaded to stay. I'd talked to the sail maker about hurricanes,

'Why you wanna sail all the way to Trinidad. Here is cool, I've been through lots of hurricanes. Look at this bay, surrounded by mountains, you'd be safe here.'

It was true that thousands of boats stay in the islands during hurricane season. It would be impossible for them all to leave and sail south. It was also true that there were some very sheltered bays. Leverick Bay for example seemed like a good place to me. However, I still thought it was a big risk to stay. Since I'd sailed all the way from Grand Cayman to get out of the zone, it didn't make sense to stay. NOAA, the National Oceanic and Atmospheric Administration, released their hurricane season forecast for 2017. It was going to be an above average year for hurricanes, five to nine was their guess.

Five months later, the BVI would be destroyed by hurricane Irma, a category five hurricane, and then hurricane Maria, another category five hurricane two weeks later. Leverick Bay, The Bitter End, Sir Richard Branson's house on Necker Island, all were devastated. The eye of the hurricane also passed over Nanny Cay and wiped out almost all the boats there.

Epilogue

I was so happy and relieved to be back in St Martin. I hadn't really been looking forward to the crossing; the Anegada Passage has a very bad reputation, and last time I did it, I had a nightmare. I left at dawn and for the first two hours struggled to get past Richard Branson's island with some very strong current, lumpy seas and wind from the southeast. I sailed through the day and night, tacked twice, dodged two very big squalls but then went right through one about eighteen miles from Marigot Bay. I finally arrived very battered and bruised; it had taken me thirty hours. I cleared in, had a pizza and a beer and went to sleep aching all over.

I had lots of boat part shopping and repairs to do. St Martin is the cheapest and easiest place to get things done, so the next day I dinghied into the lagoon and hit the chandleries. I got my mainsheet truck fixed at FKG, got my winch repaired, bought a new wind vane, new halyard, a new alternator and loads of other bits and pieces. After, I dinghied back over to Marigot Bay and went for a swim. I noticed lots of half-sunk yachts in the lagoon. Damage from Hurricane Gonzalez in 2014.

I was very tempted to stay in St Martin. I love it there, and one of my friends was working at Island Water World chandlery. The threat of hurricanes though kept me going and I reluctantly left and headed south again. Four months later, St Martin would be destroyed by hurricane Irma, as was Barbuda and the Virgin Islands. Leverick Bay, Soper's Hole and Nanny Cay, my favourite places, places I'd been only a few weeks earlier were all completely destroyed. In St Martin the eye of the storm passed over the lagoon. Over two hundred yachts were sunk spilling thousands of gallons of oil and diesel.

Two weeks after that, Dominica and Puerto Rico were destroyed by hurricane Maria. I saw films of trees being uprooted by the wind, trucks blown over and one hundred and fifty mile an hour coconuts. Then there were the post disaster photos of boats washed up onto restaurants and balconies. Shocking images of the once lush green hills now a dusty brown, stripped bare of every tree and shrub.

I had continued to Trinidad and was very glad that I did. I spent the hurricane season there watching the horror on TV in safety. I did some more teaching, hauled *Sonic Boom* out of the water and painted the hull again. After the hurricane season, I headed north and am currently anchored in Martinique.

In the future, there is still much of the Caribbean left to explore. I would like to go to Saba, the small island near St Martin. Saba is a steep sided mountain that rises out of the sea. There aren't any beaches, people there live on top of the mountain, ironically in a town called Bottom. Up in the clouds, they wear warm clothing; it's not a typical island lifestyle, more like a Caribbean Tibet. The waters around Saba are clear; it's a great place to go scuba diving, well known for sea horses. I would also like to sail to Panama, go through the canal and visit the islands of the Pacific.